The Australian Shepherd Judging Compendium
An Illustrated Workbook

Written and Illustrated
by Jeanne Joy Hartnagle-Taylor

Edited by Kristin Tara Horowitz

The Australian Shepherd Judging Compendium
An Illustrated Workbook

Copyright © 2018 Jeanne Joy Hartnagle-Taylor

All rights reserved. No part of this book may be used or reproduced in any manner whatsoever, including electronic media, Internet, or newsletters, without written permission from the publisher.

ISBN – 978-0-9898800-0-8
BISAC: PET004010 Pets / Dogs / Breeds

Printed in the United States

Table of Contents

History – Page 1
General Appearance - Page 10
Temperament / Character - Page 16
Head - Page 22
Teeth - Page 28
Eyes - Page 34
Ears - Page 40
Neck, Topline, Body – Page 44
Forequarters – Page 54
Hindquarters - Page 68
Gait - Page 80
Coat - Page 92
Color - Page 96
Size - Page 104
☑ **Judges Checklist** - Page 107

The Australian Shepherd Judging Compendium is not intended to be an exhaustive study on gait and structure. There are a number of books that already address those topics. Nevertheless, none of them talk about the kind of work Australian Shepherds actually do and the type of structure necessary to accomplish it. My hope is this workbook will help judges and non-judges gain a better understanding and appreciation for the qualities that make the Australian Shepherd unique from all other breeds. **Please note:** The quizzes in this book are not a test. They're designed to make you think. The answer may not always be straightforward. I've intentionally used the questions and answers to deepen your learning in an active way. Any of the illustrations that appear a little fuzzy are included because they provide an historical context for the breed. They are of dogs that were proven by the yardstick of performance 30 to 50 years ago. – Jeanne Joy

This book is dedicated to my dad, Ernie Hartnagle pictured (above) in 1948 on the hay meadows of the IK Barr Ranch which is now Vail Colorado.

I could have never written this workbook without my parents who inspired our family — by their example of continuous learning and their willingness to share their knowledge with others. One of my favorite memories is seeing dad measure Aussie after Aussie and then compiling the data to make this workbook possible. He often says, "Watch the withers. They hold the secret to the balance of a dog."

Foreword

Jeanne Joy Hartnagle-Taylor is my sister. She is the one who always has my best interests at heart. You will not find two people more fiercely loyal than sisters and my sister has always been my biggest ally. There is something to be said about truly growing up side by side with our working Aussies, choosing to stay close, and to continue that deep friendship into adulthood. While our preferences in Aussies occasionally differ, we never disagree on the importance of sound structure and the necessity of correct form to perform the function.

Nobody is better qualified to illustrate the Aussie in action. We grew up using these dogs in the ***real world***. From moving multitudes of sheep and cattle on the Taylor Ranch, to running livestock in commercial environments, and to handling wild Bison for the Department of Interior in Yellowstone National Park. We used our Australian Shepherds, whose instinct, training, structure and overall soundness enabled us to excel in these tasks. It was these **exact same** Australian Shepherds we showed in conformation to their championships. The very same Aussies that we successfully trialed and titled in stockdog competitions and successfully trialed and titled in obedience. Our family's breeding program, Hartnagle's Las Rocosa Aussies has earned the distinction of the first-ever Hall of Fame Kennel and the first-ever Hall of Fame Excellent Kennel. Versatility has been an expectation of our Aussies since our beginning in 1955 and continues today.

As the author of the breed's most important work, "***All About Aussies***", Jeanne Joy writes from the perspective of a breeder, a multi-disciplined judge, a successful competitor, and steward of the Australian Shepherd. Not just for judges, this work is an invaluable reference tool for anyone wanting an Aussie for a high-octane lifestyle. It provides excellent information for breeders, who bear the responsibility for matching the most suitable puppy or dog to a client's expectations. With incredibly detailed photographs and illustrations, this book reveals the structural strengths to strive for in breeding programs and the structural issues that must be taken into consideration to better understand the Aussies capabilities and limitations within the context of their structure and function.

While the growing fancy seems to popularize extremes, the true Aussie excels in the moderate. I encourage you to become more knowledgeable about the correct form and function of this amazing breed and too, become a steward of the Australian Shepherd.

– Carol Ann Hartnagle

Introduction

The content of this judging compendium goes beyond the usual discussion of dog conformation. Jeanne Joy Hartnagle-Taylor has made everything about judging dogs a specific discussion of the Australian Shepherd. This is not a "one size fits all" understanding of the generic show dog where the structure of diverse breeds is standardized into a single understanding of what is correct.

Jeanne Joy uses her lifetime of experience with the Australian Shepherd breed, and her wealth of knowledge, to give a deeper and more specific understanding of the structure of this unique breed. With a keen knowledge of the real purpose of the Aussie, Jeanne Joy takes the reader out of the world of general dog knowledge. She uses the analogy of the trotting horse compared to the sprinting horse to demonstrate this difference. It has become a popular belief that the Australian Shepherd is a trotting breed where an extended smooth trot is preferred over a more balanced and collected trot. Ms. Hartnagle-Taylor goes to great lengths to illustrate the difference between these two types of structure and is qualified to make this comparison and illustrate which is most correct to the real purpose of the working Australian Shepherd.

Ms. Hartnagle-Taylor is just the authority to make the distinctions that she has delineated throughout this book. While many accepted authorities within the broader dog world have defined a structure and gait that is popularly accepted as correct in the show world, this author takes those assumptions and suppositions to task. Jeanne Joy Hartnagle-Taylor has worked a wide variety of breeds of dogs, and countless Australian Shepherds, throughout North America and beyond. She knows what the structure of a true working Australian Shepherd should be and is sharing her superior knowledge in this text.

Overextended and sweeping trots that exaggerate the forward momentum of the dog may be pretty to look at and give multi-breed judges a standard by which to compare dogs from different breeds, but that is not correct to the real working Australian Shepherd. As a matter of fact, it is simply wrong. This type of structure destroys the agility, maneuverability, and usefulness of the working Australian Shepherd. The Australian Shepherds that developed on the farms and ranches of North America were real working dogs. Those dogs that have been distorted and bred to have extreme trotting gaits are not suited to that task. In fact, many herding trainers have lamented the, "rocking horse," action that those trotters display as they accelerate beyond the trot. That incorrect gait is often unsettling to the stock. It is certainly not suited to the efficient working of livestock. It never existed in the breed until dogs were selectively bred for the show ring.

Jeanne Joy Hartnagle-Taylor knows how incorrect structure and movement are not just superficial faults. They are out of type for the breed and detrimental to the original intended purpose of the breed. Jeanne guides the reader through this distinction as she illustrates and discusses what to look for and what is correct. Jeanne uses pictures of a wide variety of dogs that would be within the historical type of the breed. With an emphasis on the moderation described in both breed standards, one can see that moderation is essential to the real Australian Shepherd.

This compendium is a publication whose time has come. It is critical reading for anyone who takes the breeding and showing of the Australian Shepherd seriously. Those who work their Aussies in trials, and real-world settings, would do well to study this publication carefully. Real structure, movement, and type are not only critical to those judging and competing in the breed ring, but to those who want their Aussies to excel and thrive in the historical environment that created our beloved Australian Shepherds.

– Michael J. Ryan

First and foremost, the Australian Shepherd is a true working stockdog, and anything that detracts from his usefulness as such is undesirable. The most important breed characteristics are overall moderation in size and bone, balance with correct proportions, and sound movement.

— ASCA Breed Standard

Early Years

During the early years, most Aussie activity took place in the western ranch country of Arizona, California, Colorado and the Pacific Northwest.

Form Follows Function

The Australian Shepherd was developed in a time when ranches were measured in sections (square miles), not acres. Sheep outfits like the Warren Livestock Company ran 25,000 head of sheep over 284,000 acres between Casper, Wyoming and Greeley, Colorado. Ranches today can be compared to the size of a postage stamp on a football field.

The breed's foundation as a sheep and cowdog is the baseline for their structure and temperament. The breed's original purpose as a working stockdog is reflected in its over-all type.

Jay Sisler with Shorty (1948 – 1959) on the left and Stub (1948 – 1960) on the right.

Prior to the 1970s

During the early 1950s and 60s, Jay Sisler, a rancher and rodeo contestant from Idaho was the first to introduce Australian Shepherds to the public. Jay and his dogs delighted rodeo audiences throughout the United States and Canada with an array of tricks that have yet to be equaled even today. In fact, so unique and delightful were these dogs that Walt Disney Studios produced two movies featuring them: **Stub, The World's Greatest Cowdog**, and **Run Appaloosa, Run.**

Fletcher Wood's dogs, Hartnagle's Las Rocosa line and the ancestry of many present-day Aussies.

Stub and Shorty jumping rope at the National Western Stock Show and Rodeo in 1954. Shorty sitting on Stub below at the Boulder Pow Wow rodeo in 1955.

Jay pictured with Stub and Shorty performing their signature act above.

Any serious breeder or judge must see these movies especially, **Stub: Best Cowdog in the West.** Why? Because it is a visual history of the breed type and the character of the foundation dogs. The film features Jay Sisler's dogs performing their trademark tricks as well as working a formidable 1,800-pound horned Brahma bull.

Shorty figures prominently in the early bloodlines including Juanita Ely's dogs, Weldon T. Heard's Flintridge bloodlines,

Sisler's Silver pictured in *Run Appaloosa, Run* in 1967.

Ely's Blue, a littermate to Sisler's Queenie and one of the early foundation bitches of the breed.

A Glimpse at Some Early Show Dogs

Prior to early 1975, breed activity was limited to the western states, mainly Arizona, California, Colorado, Idaho and the Pacific Northwest. The only organized activities available for the breed to earn titles were Conformation, Obedience and Tracking events. The ASCA Stockdog Program was in the works.

Here is a small sample of some of the early Aussies that were exhibited in the conformation ring from the 1960s to 1970s. Notice the moderate length hair coats:

Roadrunner's Picacho. DOB: 1966.

Early in the breed's history, a large number of the show dogs were actual working dogs. Aussies shown in the conformation ring were the same dogs that were handling livestock at home for their owners.

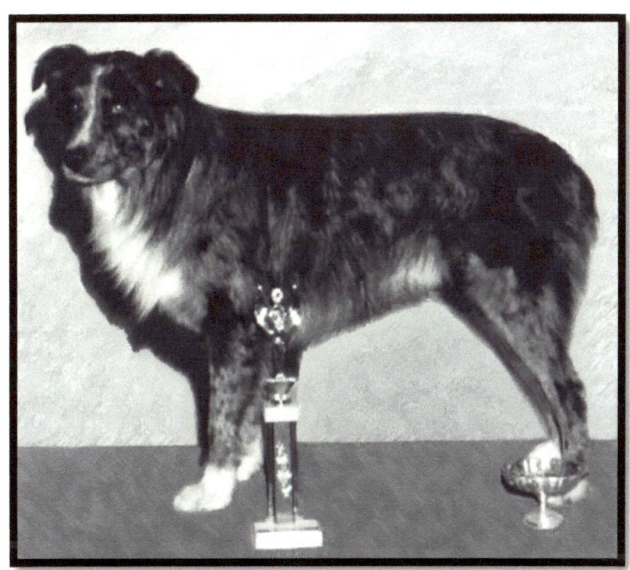

Rowe's Comanche Warrior STD-s,c RD. DOB: 1967.

ASCA's first Champion of record, HOF Champion Wildhagen's Dutchman of Flintridge CDX. DOB: 1969.

HOF Champion Fieldmaster of Flintridge CDX. DOB: 1969.

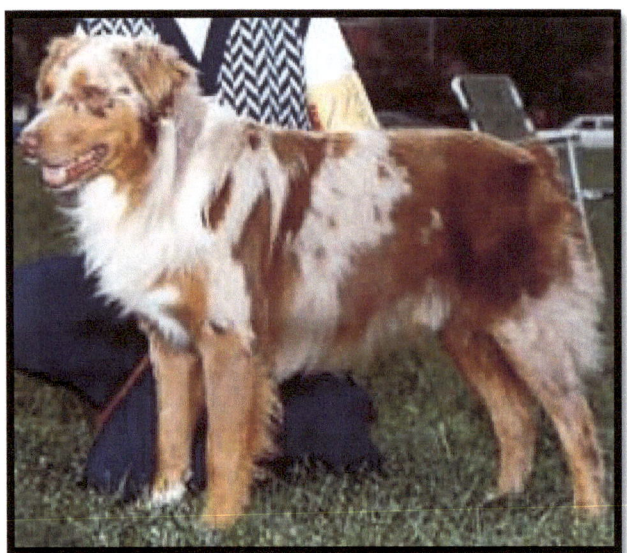

HOF sire, George's Red Rustler. DOB: 1969.

HOF Champion Las Rocosa Shiloh CD. DOB 1970.

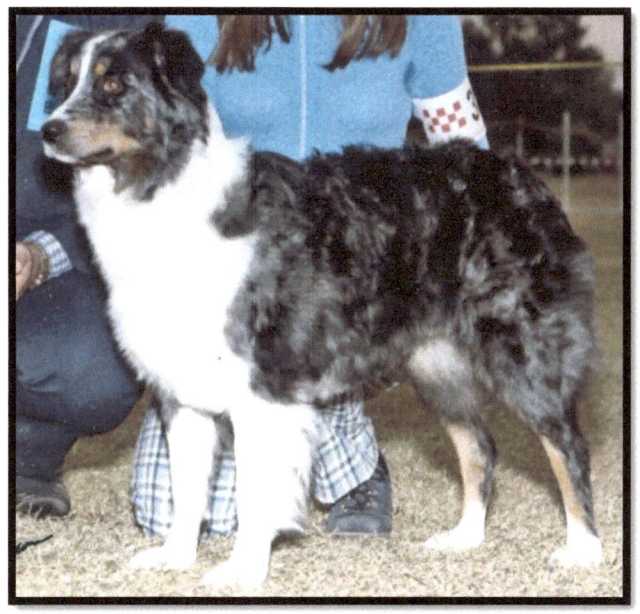
Shank's Ginks of Coppertone. DOB: 1970.

Champion Shanahan's Phantom CDX. DOB: 1971.

Las Rocosa Cherokee Chica. DOB: 1971.

HOF Champion Hemi's Regal Request CD, STD-s, OTD-d. DOB: 1972.

HOF Champion Windermere's Sunshine of Bonnie-Blu, CDX. DOB: 1975.

HOF Champion Copper Canyon Caligari CD. DOB: 1973.

Champion Just Jake of Las Rocosa CD, ATD-d, OTD-s, STD-c. DOB: 1978.

HOF Champion Chulo Rojo of Fairoaks CD. DOB: 1975.

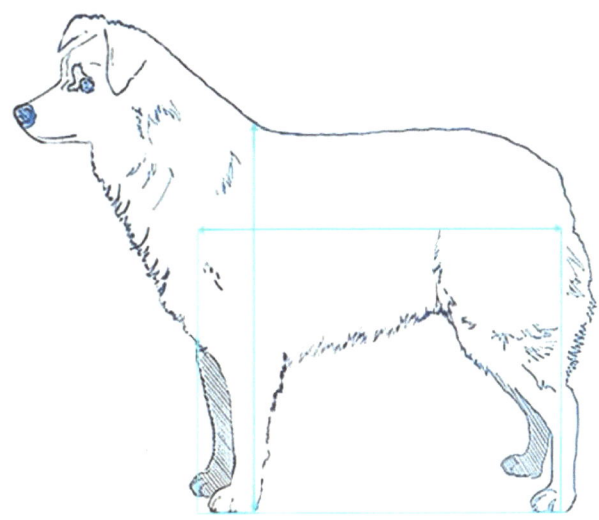

Architecture of the Breed

The yardstick of performance was the original blueprint used as the guideline to preserve the breed's function as an upright working dog. That's the lens we must look at the breed standard through.

The Australian Shepherd is **not** a sustained trotting breed as some people mistakenly believe. Aussies must be able to turn swiftly in order to keep stock together as well as overtake and bring back any animals that split and run from the group.

In the real-world, Aussies may have to trot on rough ground, through heavy snow and deep sand or thick mud, unlike their cousins who trot on level surfaces in a show ring. The breed's original, historic function is as a quick and agile working stockdog.

The Breed's Changing Structure

In 1977, ASCA (Australian Shepherd Club of America) adopted the breed standard that was in use for over 30 years. In that period of time, we have seen a distinct kind of Aussie emerge from the early foundation ranch dogs with the original sprinting structure. The standard aided by the show program saw the development of an Australian Shepherd with the trotting drive train.

What does that mean for the breed? Not all Australian Shepherds are created equal. Although most Aussies have the same basic appearance that sets them apart from other breeds, there is a distinct difference between the basic structure and trotting style of the working and the show bloodlines. A comparison can be drawn between the differences of the working Quarter Horse and the trotting Standardbred in their natural gaits.

Ernest Hartnagle, one of the drafters of the original ASCA 1977 Breed Standard said, "The development of the trotting Aussie produced a dog that could move effortlessly for long distances. The trade-off for this development was paid for with the sacrifice of supreme agility necessary to outrun and turn sheep and cattle. The longer extension of gait naturally produces a slower reaction time to negotiate changes of direction." A dog with the trotting drive train requires an extra stride to alter gaits or change direction.

Sprinting Drivetrain	Trotting Drivetrain
Moderate shoulder with a seemingly shorter upper arm. A little less slope to front pasterns.	More shoulder layback and return of upper arm with more slope to the front pasterns.
More fast twitch muscles, (heavier muscles).	More slow twitch muscles, (longer, leaner muscles).
Hind legs are more under the pelvis.	Hind legs are out behind pelvis.
Steeper croup	**Flatter croup**
Longer hocks (Metatarsi).	**Shorter hocks** (Metatarsi).
Shorter, quicker strides at the trot.	Longer strides at the trot.
Aussies with the sprinting drivetrain are more exact when placing their feet and are able to turn more sharply than Aussies with greater angulation.	Aussies with the trotting drivetrain are able to take longer strides with their legs covering more ground but are slower making gait changes.
Forward, ground covering running style.	**Up and down running style like a rocking horse.**

To reiterate, the greater angulation of the drivetrain built for sustained trotting produces fewer strides per 100 feet than the sprinting drivetrain does at the same gait. In other words, while the trotter is in the process of completing the first stride, the sprinter is in it's second stride. The trotting dog spends more time in the air due to the longer stride which produces a slower reaction time. The sprinter, however, with his shorter stride is more agile and can make abrupt changes in direction much quicker.

Sorting, penning, and turning back livestock often requires rapid accelerations, sharp turns, abrupt stops at full speed and roll backs, simultaneously changing leads and be at a "flat out" run again in two strides in a different direction (using the inside lead next to the critter). As well as dodging flying hooves and lethal horns. This primary work cannot be accomplished with the sustained trotting style that is enhanced through show ring pageantry, but must be accomplished at different gaits from a walk to a "sprint."

Performance Aussies also depend on the sprinting drivetrain for maximum efficiency in Agility, Flyball, Frisbee and every other activity that requires quickness, good jumping ability, and turn around efficiency.

If we stop looking at the Australian Shepherd through the lens of its original purpose as a working stockdog, we will have created (in time) a distinctly different breed.

The Standard of Excellence – The Ideal

The Australian Shepherd is a performance breed. Conformation and temperament affect every Aussie's ability to perform. An Aussie that doesn't have sound structure will never realize its full potential, nor will he function effectively as a healthy, sound working dog.

The breed standard is the model toward which all Australian Shepherd breeders strive. Written by people who knew the dogs firsthand in the environment where they were originally developed, the breed standard is blueprint for judges to evaluate against. The philosophy underlying the manner in which such a document should be written was best described by Dr. Robert Kline, DVM:

"Contrary to the beliefs of many, such a standard is not a textbook but rather an outline describing structure, breed characteristics, color, size, uses, etc. put down in as precise and accurate a manner as possible. In order to perfect a document without in fact ending up with a textbook the size of a physician's anatomy book, it is predisposed that the people using such a standard have a working knowledge of animal traits, vocabulary, and methods used by the industry to enable them to understand and interpret said standard so as to make it a usable instrument. For those not so familiar with these things and wanting to use the standard, such persons owe it to themselves to seek out knowledgeable breeders and judges, texts, etc. to avail themselves of such knowledge. For accuracy's sake, it precludes a standard to be written for the beginner or novice."

Newcomers to the breed may have a difficult time comprehending the basis on which a judge evaluates each dog. The Australian Shepherd breed standard describes an ideal Australian Shepherd in terms familiar to individuals who understand canine terminology, and it assumes a basic knowledge of anatomy and gait. It is not a detailed layout, nor is it a breeding manual for the novice, but it provides guidelines within which breeders can work without compromising with popular fads.

It is understood that variation from the ideal is to be faulted according to the extent it departs from the ideal. Points that diverge significantly from breed character or soundness are faulted severely. Characteristics that entirely detract from both soundness and/or breed character are disqualifications.

Most references to measurements compare one part to another, and all parts to the whole individual Aussie, rather than by specific numerical increments. By doing so, slight variations in size of respective segments are allowed when comparing several Aussies that differ in overall size. This also emphasizes the importance of each part being in proportion to one another, therefore maintaining balance and symmetry.

The ideal *Australian Shepherd* is *found* **not** in the extremes, but his *excellence is found* in the *balance between the extremes.*

 ## General Appearance

 ## General Appearance

The Australian Shepherd is an intelligent working dog of strong herding and guarding instincts. He is a loyal companion and has the stamina to work all day. He is well balanced, slightly longer than tall, of medium size and bone, with coloring that offers variety and individuality. He is attentive and animated, lithe and agile, solid and muscular without cloddiness. He has a coat of moderate length and coarseness. He has a docked or natural bobbed tail.

The Australian Shepherd is a well-balanced dog of medium size and bone. He is attentive and animated, showing strength and stamina combined with unusual agility. Slightly longer than tall, he has a coat of moderate length and coarseness with coloring that offers variety and individuality in each specimen. An identifying characteristic is his natural or docked bobtail. In each sex, masculinity or feminity is well defined.

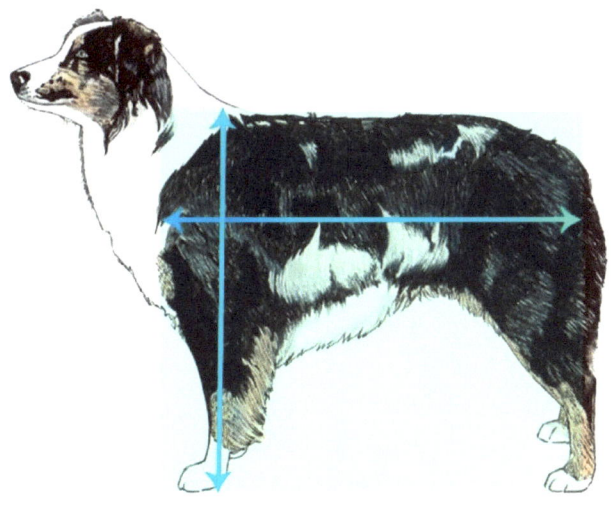

"Slightly longer than tall" is measured from the withers to the ground and then from the point of shoulder to the point of buttock.

Form Follows Function

Aussies were built to sprint and stop suddenly at full speed, roll back, change leads, and in two strides be again at a sprint in another direction. The breed's slightly longer than tall physique contributes greatly to this ability. It's critical for the type of work they were originally developed for.

Unusual agility is typical of Australian Shepherds and necessary for stockdogs.

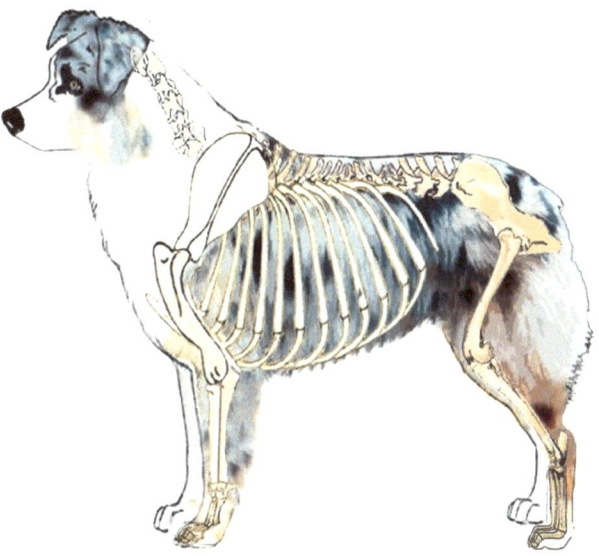

Several words, "medium," "moderate," and "balanced," describe what to look for in a well-proportioned individual. Aussies are medium size dogs with medium bone. Medium size and bone refers to the overall size of the dog and skeletal structure, the underpinning of the breed's conformation.

The average sized Aussie with moderate bone is ideal. Some people mistakenly believe large boned Aussies are less prone to injury than those with smaller bone.

Research at the College of Veterinary Medicine at MSU found dogs with big bone had less bone mineral density than dogs with smaller bone. In other words, their bones are more fragile and prone to injury. In fact, the more moderate boned dogs tended to have higher bone-mineral density and a larger ratio of the bones were dense from the hollow core to the outer layer. The study was based on spines and the long (limb) bones using x-rays and computed tomography (CT). **Heavy dogs are also slower to accelerate and make turns.**

Cattle can be dangerous to work. Aussies take a lot of hard knocks. They are managing animals that weigh ten times what they do.

As a genuine athlete, Aussies are agile, never cumbersome nor carrying extra timber. **In a nutshell**, Aussies are not draft animals. They are not supposed to be strong boned dogs like the Bernese Mountain Dog. Nor should they be spindly and fine boned.

The ideal Australian Shepherd has neither one outstanding feature nor any glaring faults that would distract from the total picture of symmetry. An ideal specimen will stand out in harmonious balance at rest or while in motion. He blends from one point to another.

The Aussie should convey the impression at a glance that he is capable of enduring long periods of active duty as a stockdog, which is attributed to his strength and stamina. He is light on his feet.

From heading to heeling to dodging a kick, the breed was developed as a working stockdog able to handle a variety of livestock.

There is a distinguishable difference between males and females. Although never coarse or menacing, the male's boldness and virile strength are easy to distinguish from his distinctly feminine counterpart, who possesses structural equality and a definite strength of character.

Variety and individuality in color are unique features of Aussies. The natural or docked bobtail is an identifying characteristic. The variance in tail length accommodates the different lengths that occur naturally at birth. The longer natural bobtail (not to exceed four inches) should never be penalized over a shorter natural bobbed or docked tail.

Aussies being exhibited in countries where tail docking bans exist should not be faulted for having a tail longer than four (4) inches.

Test Your Judging I.Q. General Appearance

1. ☐ True ☐ False. Breed standards assume the reader has a basic knowledge of canine anatomy.

2. Since the Australian Shepherd is a herding/working breed the judge must:

  a. Place emphasis on structure and movement over breed type.
  b. Not place too much emphasis on any one feature.
  c. Look at the dog as a whole.
  d. All the above.

3. An identifying characteristic of the Australian Shepherd is its:

  a. Square frame.
  b. Eyes of two different colors.
  c. Natural or docked bobtail.
  d. Stoic expression.

4. ☐ AKC ☐ ASCA. Body length is measured from the prosternum to the point of buttock or pin bone.

5. The breed's overall body shape indicates it is built for:

  a. Endurance trotting.
  b. Agility and sprinting.
  c. Strength and stamina combined with unusual agility.

6. What determines the correct body shape for the Australian Shepherd?

  a. Hock length.

    b. Shape of the feet.
    c. Ratio of height to length.
    d. All the above.

7. ☐ AKC or ☐ ASCA. Structure in the male reflects masculinity without coarseness.

8. ☐ AKC or ☐ ASCA. Bitches appear feminine without being slight of bone.

9. ☐ True ☐ False. There is a recognizable difference between the basic structure of Aussies with the sprinting drivetrain and Aussies with the trotting drivetrain.

10. The Australian Shepherd is agile and

    a. Able to make instantaneous gait changes.
    b. Ready to work in all situations.
    c. Ready to protect his/her master.
    d. Able to endure all types of weather.
    e. All the above.

11. The adult Australian Shepherd is traditionally shown:

    a. On the table.
    b. Hand-stacked.
    c. Free-stacked.

12. ☐ True ☐ False. The length of an Aussie's leg must be in proportion to the spine.

13. Which term(s) best describe(s) the Australian Shepherd?

    a. Elegant.
    b. Athletic.
    c. Heavy.
    d. Low to the ground.

14. ☐ True ☐ False. Originators of the ASCA Breed Standard operated on the guideline of measuring body length from the point of shoulder to the pin bone also known as the point of buttock (ischium).

General Appearance Answers

1- True.

2- c. Look at the dog as a whole.

3- c. Natural or docked bobtail.

4- AKC.

5- c. Strength and stamina combined with unusual agility.

6- d. All the above.

7- AKC.

8- AKC.

9- True. Australian Shepherds from working bloodlines tend to have less shoulder layback (less slant compared to the vertical plane), a little steeper croup, longer pelvis, longer hocks a shorter, quick stride than their show counterparts built for sustained trotting.

10- e. All the above. One of the breed's hallmarks is his ability to turn sharply and make instantaneous gait changes.

11- b and c. Puppies are sometimes presented on a table making it easier for a judge to examine them, but adult Aussies are free-stacked or hand-stacked in a natural four-square stance.

12- True. The amount to which a dog's legs are shortened relative to the length of its spine, can have an overall effect on its health if the long bones of the limbs fail to grow to a normal, proportional length.

13- b. Australian Shepherds are supposed to be athletic. Individuals that are cloddy, bulky or heavy are not good representatives of the breed.

14- True.

Notes

Notes

 ## Temperament

 ## Character

The Australian Shepherd is an intelligent, active dog with an even disposition; he is good natured, seldom quarrelsome. He may be somewhat reserved in initial meetings. *Faults* – Any display of shyness, fear or aggression is to be severely penalized.

From the **General Appearance**: The Australian Shepherd is an intelligent working dog of strong herding and guarding instincts.

The Australian Shepherd is primarily a working dog of strong herding and guardian instincts. He is an intelligent, exceptional companion. He is versatile and easily trained: performing his assigned tasks with great style and enthusiasm. He is reserved with strangers but does not exhibit shyness. This unusually versatile stockdog works with the power and quickness to control difficult cattle as well as the ability to move sheep without unnecessary roughness. Although an aggressive, authoritative worker, viciousness toward people or animals is intolerable.

The Breed's Personality

Without the Australian Shepherd's extraordinary abilities, herding large bands of sheep on the western ranges would have been nearly impossible. Especially when you consider the conditions that the dogs worked under: sheep are able to forage on land with sparse plant life too arid to support other types of livestock. They are exposed to all weather and wild-life often in remote locations.

Numerous are the tales of an Aussie saving the lives of herder and the sheep from wild animals or snowstorms. Had it not been for the Aussie's determination and sensible nature, neither the sheep nor herder would have survived. For example, one day, our herder suffered a heart attack while out on the range. Our little Goody (Hartnagle's Goodie) watched over him and guarded him for three days (without food or water) and protected him from predators. She kept the buzzards from pecking out his eyes. Goody who was typical of the early dogs. Her demeanor was pleasant. She was a delightful babysitter and kind with children and young animals. She was a sensible guardian, quiet and courageous, yet highly responsive and obedient.

Wood's Dandy, a foundation sire, was outwardly protective. He had to be to defend his flock of sheep and herder from bears and other predators. On one occasion, Dandy was scalped by a bear trying to kill some sheep. He didn't quit protecting his flock until the bear was no longer a threat. Had he been socialized in a modern world, there's no doubt he would have been considered child safe. Though, he was calm and stable he would not have been suitable for the pet market. He was a tough dog.

His granddaughter, Heard's Blue Spice was an ambassador for the breed. She was lovely and very pleasant. Yet one night, after office hours, a man walked in Dr. Heard's vet clinic in Denver, Colorado. The man insisted his dog needed medical attention and wanted Dr. Heard to administer medication.

After examining the dog, Dr. Heard didn't find anything wrong with her and explained she was fine and didn't need medical care. The man, who had been drinking, became belligerent and insisted that Doc give her a shot. With inebriated reasoning, he became threatening.

About that time, Blue Spice (above) who had been waiting quietly in the back sailed over the opened Dutch door into the examining room. The man was immediately convinced that Doc was right. When Dr. Heard called her off, she responded just as quickly and sat quietly by his feet. This is the type of sagacity (the ability to discern when and how to protect) the breed was founded on.

From being faithful family companions to stock savvy stockdogs, the Australian Shepherd is a highly versatile farm and ranch dog.

Aussies have to be smart and tough to work hard-hitting cattle that when full grown can weigh an average of 1,500 pounds.

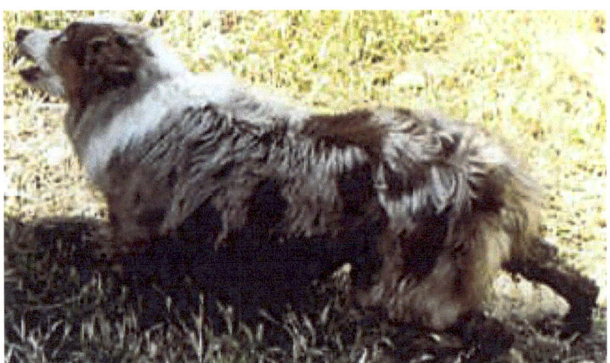

In the above close-up, notice how the dog is looking up at the cow to see which leg is carrying the weight to avoid being kicked.

As tough as Aussies have to be with cattle and formidable black face rams....

...they can be equally gentle with poultry.

One of the breed's hallmarks is its ability to handle young goats and ewes with lambs with finesse.

Working hogs takes courage and stock savvy because hogs are highly intelligent and can bite back.

Australian Shepherds are extremely agile. They can jump high, run hard and chase a ball with the speed of greased lightning. They are natural stockdogs with strong herding instincts and naturally work in close proximity to their livestock. They are extremely intelligent and adapt readily to a multitude of different tasks and situations.

Aussies have to be quick to follow commands, but also must be able to think and act on their own since they sometimes work out of sight of their master.

Aussies are natural guardians. They are territorial and protective, but not vicious.

Although an aggressive, authoritative worker, Aussies are kind to their charges.

Aussies are extremely loyal and willing to please their masters, which is evident by their eagerness to respond. Australian Shepherds are people oriented but reserved with strangers.

Test Your Judging I.Q. Character / Temperament

1. The Australian Shepherd is known as a

   a. Robust little dog able to trot long distances.
   b. Strong, powerful dog able to trot all day.
   c. Athletic, medium dog with stamina to work all day.
   d. An authoritative worker.

2. What does "Reserved with strangers" mean?

   a. Laid-back.
   b. Shy.
   c. Watchful.
   d. Uneasy.

3. ☐ ASCA ☐ AKC. Any display of shyness, fear or aggression is to be severely penalized.

4. ☐ True ☐ False. The Australian Shepherd's temperament is much like the Golden Retriever.

5. ☐ True ☐ False. Strong herding and guarding instinct is an integral part of the breed's character.

6. ☐ ASCA ☐ AKC. Any display of shyness, fear or aggression is to be faulted according to the degree of deviation.

7. ☐ True ☐ False. Although an aggressive, authoritative worker, viciousness towards people or other animals by unwarranted or unprovoked attacks are intolerable.

8. ☐ True ☐ False. Aussies are watchful in a new environment which may cause them to be timid or shy.

9. Which of the following statement(s) is/are <u>not</u> generally used to describe the Australian Shepherd breed?

   a. Aussies are natural guardians.
   b. Aussies have a reserved, stately presence.
   c. Aussies are territorial.
   d. Aussies are self-willed **and brave**.

Character / Temperament Answers

1-c. The Australian Shepherd is an athletic dog of medium build with stamina to work all day.

2-c. The Aussie may be reserved and watchful with strangers or in a new environment, but he is not fearful or shy.

3-AKC. Any display of shyness, fear or aggression is to be severely penalized.

4-False. There are some books that liken the Australian Shepherd's temperament to the Golden Retriever, but it's an erroneous comparison.

5-True.

6-ASCA. Any display of shyness or fear is to be faulted according to the degree of deviation.

7-True.

8-False. Aussies are on the alert in a new environment, but not timid or shy.

9-b and / or d.

Notes

Notes

 ## Head

 ## Head

The *Head* is clean cut, strong and dry. Overall size should be in proportion to the body. The muzzle is equal in length or slightly shorter than the back skull. Viewed from the side the topline of the back skull and muzzle form parallel planes, divided by a moderate, well-defined stop. The muzzle tapers little from base to nose and is rounded at the tip. *Skull* – Top flat to slightly domed. It may show a slight occipital protuberance. Length and width are equal. Moderate well-defined stop.

The head is clean-cut, strong, dry, and in proportion to the body. The topskull is flat to slightly rounded; its length and width each equal to the length of the muzzle. The muzzle is of medium width and depth and tapers gradually to a rounded tip, without appearing heavy or snipey. Lips are close fitting, meeting at the mouthline. The toplines of the muzzle and topskull appear close to parallel. The stop is moderate but well defined.

Dog's heads are divided into two parts, the top or backskull (cranium) and the foreface (front portion of the skull). The shape of the Aussie's head is moderate. The medium length muzzle is in proportion to the medium width and length of the topskull. It's classified as a **Mesocephalic** skull.

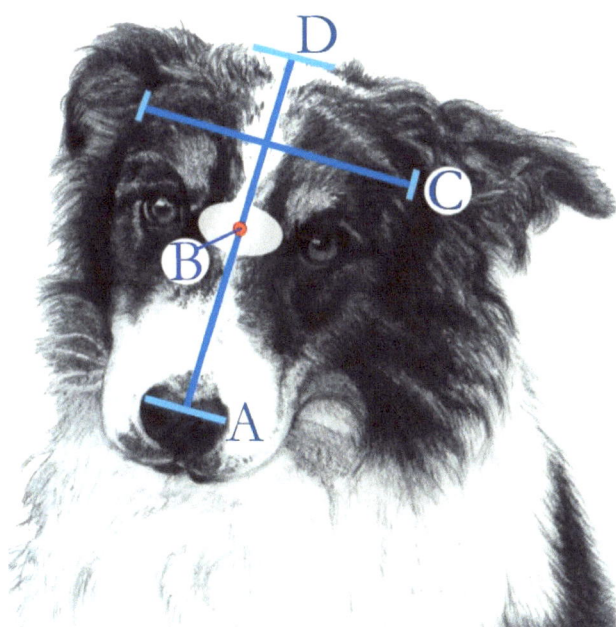

The head is measured from the tip of the nose **(A)** to the middle of the stop **(B)** — the depression in front of the eyes between the skull and the muzzle. Then from **(B)** to the occiput **(D)**. The final measurement is the width of the topskull which is measured side to side **(C)**.

The framework of the head houses the brain, dentition, ears, eyes and nose (sinus chambers). The structure protects and minimizes the effects of injury to the special senses: sight, hearing, scent, and the brain. The formation of the sinus chambers adds structural stability to the frame without adding extra weight, which is important in respiration. These chambers lend moderate width to the head, which is necessary for adequate muscle attachment. The ridge (sagittal crest) on the top skull allows for the attachment of muscles used for biting. It further affords protection from a blow to the top of the head.

A perfect example of a clean cut, dry head pictured above. The lips are close fitting

(fitting tightly) meeting at the mouth line. Note the appropriate amount of underjaw.

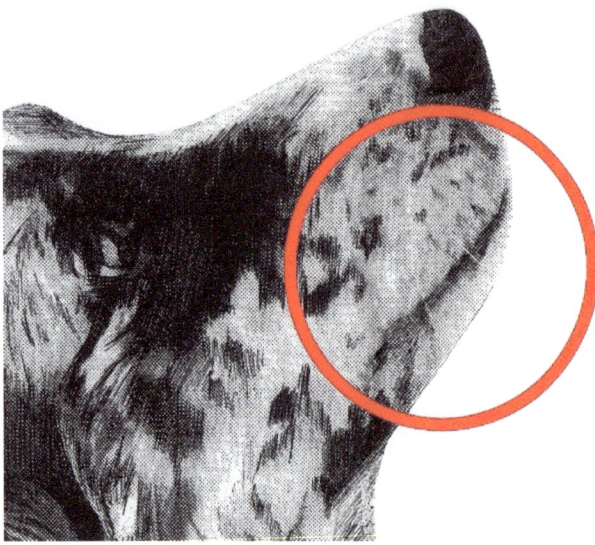

Clean-cut – Clearly outlined, well formed, trim, and neat; free from extra or loose skin, pads of fat, pendulous lips (flews), and / or visible haws (third eyelid or membrane on the inside corner of the eye). The lips must be snug and <u>not</u> hang below the line of mouth. The skin should fit well around the eye to form a tight, protective covering. This helps prevent debris (dirt, briars, seeds, brush, twigs) from making direct contact with the eyeballs. Loose-fitting lips are faulted.

A moderate, but well-defined stop (illustrated above). The muzzle tapers gradually to a rounded tip without appearing heavy nor snipy which lacks substance to the underjaw which in turn can impact dentition.

AKC	ASCA
The muzzle is equal in length or slightly shorter than the back skull.	The length of muzzle is equal to the length and width of the topskull.
Muzzle tapers little from base to nose and is rounded at the tip.	The muzzle tapers gradually to a rounded tip.

One of the main reasons you see a drastic variation in head types between ASCA and AKC are described in the head sections.

When you shorten the muzzle as is acceptable by the AKC standard there is a greater risk for tooth crowding. Dogs with shorter faces have reduced and restricted air passages in the muzzle. They are more prone to heat stress in hot humid conditions than "normal" or medium faced dogs. Breathing problems reduce stamina and a myriad of other health complications which is contrary to soundness and the purpose for which the breed was originally intended.

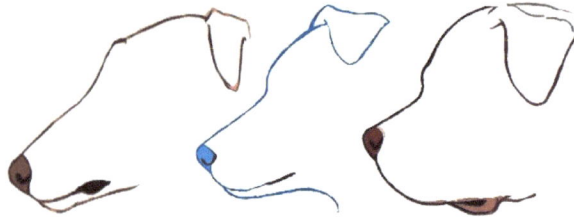

Left: Dolichocephalic (Collie, Greyhound, Saluki), **Middle:** Mesocephalic also known as a Mesaticephalic (Aussie). **Right:** Brachycephalic (Rottweiler).

In a nutshell: The Aussie's head should not resemble the short-muzzled Rottweiler nor the elongated head of the Collie.

Test Your Judging I.Q. Head

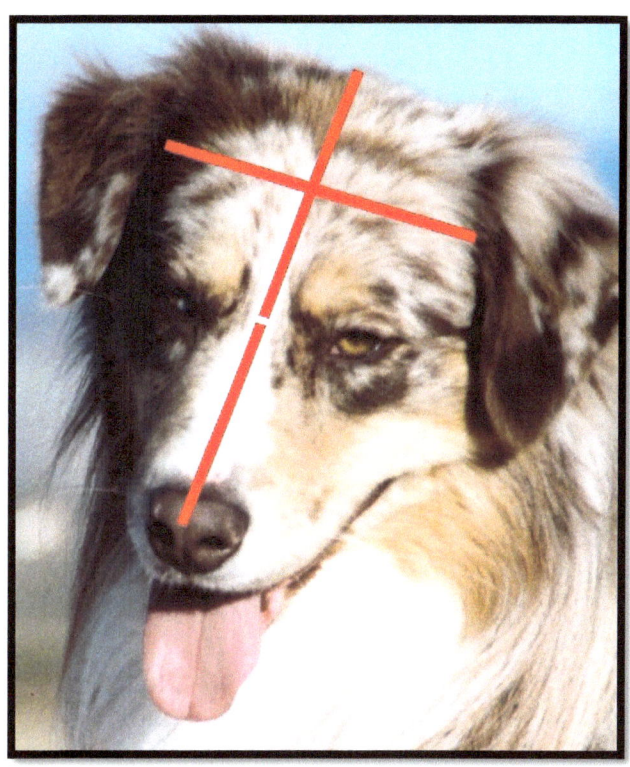

1. Match above parts of the head above:

A.   Topskull
B.   Occiput
C.   Stop
D.   Muzzle
E.   Tip of nose

2. The topskull and muzzle pictured on the above head study are on:

    a. Parallel planes.
    b. Oblique (non-parallel) planes.

3. Why is the length and width of topskull used as a guideline for length of muzzle?

    a. For tradition
    b. To keep the head from becoming too long and narrow
    c. To keep the head in proportion to the body
    d. For balance

4. ☐ True   ☐ False. The canine bite is considered part of the digestive system.

5. The muzzle tapers little from the base to nose and is:

    a. Blunt at the tip.
    b. Rounded at the tip.
    c. Pointed at the tip.

6. ☐ True   ☐ False. The head is equidistant from the width and length of the topskull to the length of the muzzle.

7. ☐ True   ☐ False. The Australian Shepherd is a dry mouth breed. Flews are untypical of the Australian Shepherd.

8. ☐ True ☐ False. Clean-cut means the Aussie's lips are close fitting, meeting at the mouthline.

> ## Head
> ## Answers

1-
A. Tip of Nose.
B. Stop.
C. Topskull.
D. Occiput.
E. Muzzle.

2-b. Oblique (non-parallel). While it may appear the the muzzle and topskull lie on parallel planes, close examination reveals this to be untypical.

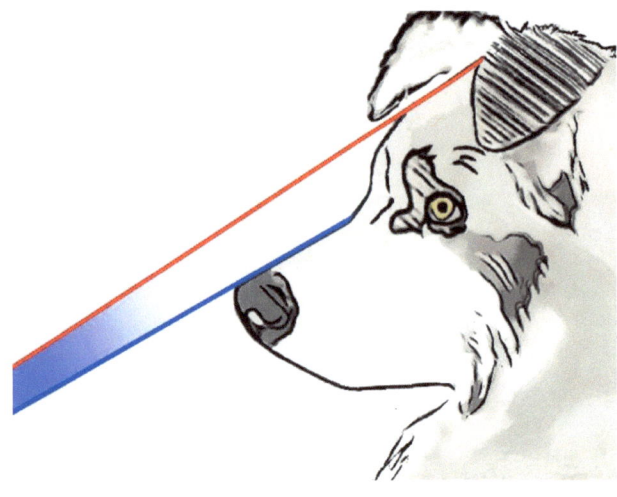

The top portion of the skull slants or slopes very slightly towards the muzzle. The slope or gradient of the topskull, the occiput to the stop (**red line**) when extended will eventually intersect with the dark **blue line** of the muzzle (the stop to the tip of the nose). By contrast parallel lines remain the same distance apart and will not meet, no matter how far you extend them.

Due to the slight tapering of the muzzle, these two features are set slightly oblique (especially if the skull is slightly domed as described by AKC), unlike breeds such as setters and pointers which also sport square, blunt muzzles, abrupt stops, and a prominent brow.

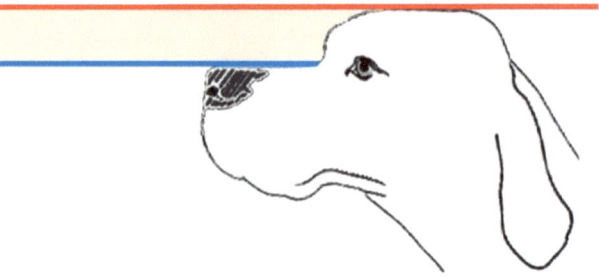

Parallel planes (illustrated above).

3-b. As breeds evolve, one of the first things to change is the head. To keep the head in correct proportions and from becoming too long and narrow or blunt it's important for the length of the muzzle be equidistant to the length and width of topskull.

4-True. However, the AKC standard allows for a shorter muzzle which changes the balance of the head from an intermediate shape to shortened Brachycephalic shape. It contributes to a blockier head shape.

5-b. Muzzle tapers gradually to a rounded tip. It's supposed to be a wedge shape.

6- True.

7-True. The Australian Shepherd should **NOT** have flews to any degree.

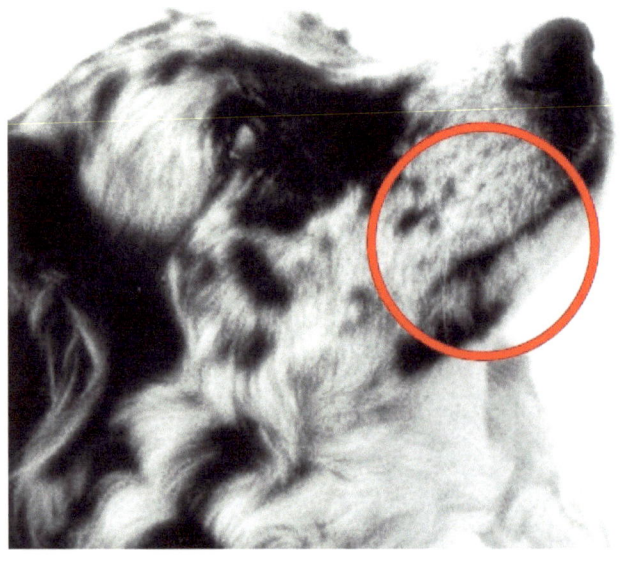

8- True. The Aussie's lips are supposed to be close fitting, meeting at the mouthline **without** flews or pendulous upper lips.

Notes

Notes

 ## Teeth

 ## Teeth

A full complement of strong white teeth should meet in a scissors bite or may meet in a level bite. Loss of contact caused by short center incisors in an otherwise correct bite shall not be judged undershot. Teeth broken or missing by accident shall not be penalized.

Disqualifications: Undershot. Overshot greater than 1/8 inch

A full complement of strong white teeth meet in a scissors bite. A level bite is a fault. Teeth broken or missing by accident are not penalized. All other missing teeth should be faulted to the degree that they deviate from a full complement of 42 teeth.

Disqualifications: Undershot bite, Overshot bite, Wry Mouth

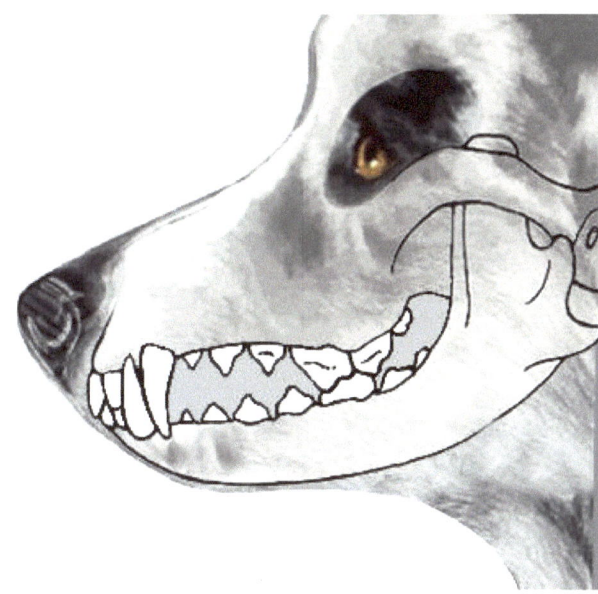

The scissors bite is anatomically correct and the most functional bite for stockdogs. It's indicative of a sound jaw assembly. It augments the slightly tapered muzzle.

Digestion begins with the teeth. Dogs with misaligned teeth (a dental malocclusion) are not able to chew food into fine enough particles for proper digestion, which will affect their overall health and stamina. To correctly evaluate the bite, we must examine all the teeth in relation to one another and to the jaw. Tooth placement is affected by the jaw structure.

The scissors bite lends substance and support to the face and dentition. It enables the Aussie to "grip" livestock with a pinching effect and be able to withstand the impact if kicked while working. The scissors bite is also necessary for removing burrs and the like from foot pads and the coat. During birth, the female must be able to sever the umbilical cord after each puppy whelped.

Each type of tooth has a specific function. The incisors (located at the center of each dental arch) are vitally important for picking up food, removing stickers from the feet, cutting umbilical cords during whelping, and many other tasks. The large, deeply rooted canine teeth set farther back in the mouth are for tearing and puncturing. The premolars (bicuspids) have two points for shearing and shredding, and the large molars are for grinding and crushing.

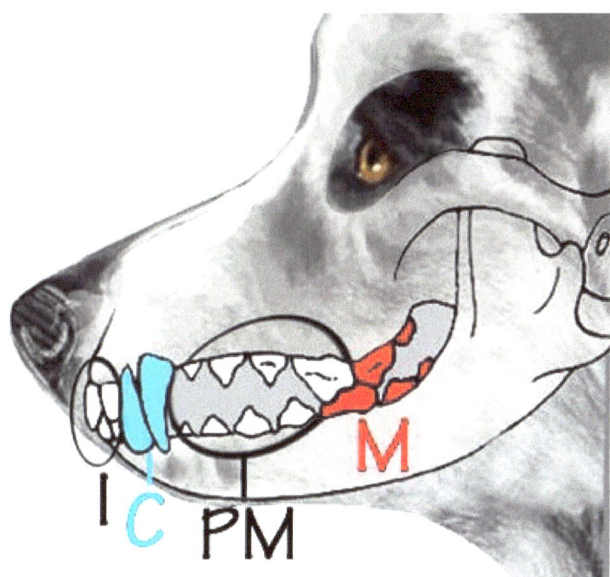

Above: **I**- Incisors, **C**- Canines, **PM**- Pre-molars, **M**- Molars.

The above illustration shows a full complement of 42 teeth in a normal scissors bite. The top or maxillary has six incisors (central, intermediate, and corner), two canine teeth, eight premolars and four molars. The bottom or mandible is exactly the same plus it has two (2) additional molars.

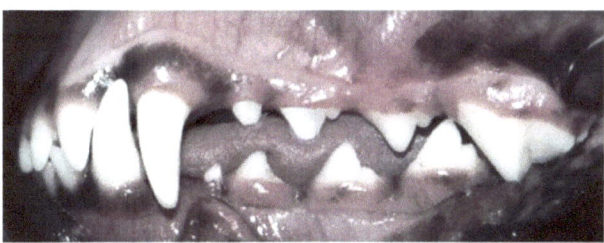
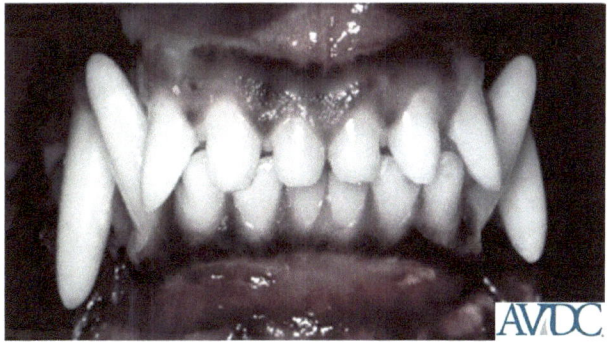

Top: Normal scissors bite. **Bottom:** Normal interplay between the top and bottom incisors (central) and canine teeth (outer).

29

The bite cannot be accurately judged by examining the incisors alone. The incisors can shift through trauma or surgery. The relationship of the canine or "fang" teeth – how they meet – is one good reference point for determining if the bite is correct. The lower canine teeth should interlock symmetrically in front of the upper canine teeth and fit at an equal distance between the outermost upper incisors. The remaining teeth should be aligned accordingly. When the lower incisors fail to meet the inside top of the upper incisors causing a gap is highly detrimental to the breed's health and function.

When viewed from the side of the dog's mouth, the upper and lower premolars should interdigitate; that is, the lower first premolar sits in front of the upper first premolar, and the rest of the upper and lower premolars alternate in sawtooth fashion. Overall, the premolars should give the appearance of a pinking shear.

AKC
Loss of contact caused by short center incisors in an otherwise correct bite shall not be judged undershot.

Loss of contact by center incisors is not an undershot bite **as long as** the relationship of the upper and lower jaw is normal and the canine and premolar teeth on both sides of the mouth are normally aligned. It is faulted however because the teeth are not seated soundly in the mandible. The central incisors are not well rooted in the jaw bone therefore more vulnerable to trauma.

AKC	ASCA
Teeth **should** meet in a scissors bite **or** may meet in a level bite.	A level bite is a fault.

Level or Even Bite

When the lower jaw shifts forward, the bite is known as a level bite, in which the incisors meet edge to edge. The interplay between the lower canine tooth and outermost upper incisor and between the upper canine tooth and the lower and upper premolar cusp tips are all affected, according to the degree of shift. The more the bottom jaw shifts forward, the greater the tendency toward occlusal trauma (broken, chipped, abnormal and unevenly worn teeth). The excessive and uneven wear on the upper and lower incisors erodes the teeth during normal chewing, eventually exposing the root canal.

The forward position of the jaw leaves the mandible more prone to injury because it is less protected. The mandible is more vulnerable because it attaches to the head in one place only; therefore, the force cannot be dispersed when the mandible is subjected to trauma.

The level is faulted in ASCA because it's a genetically abnormal occlusion. AKC doesn't fault it even though it's a type of undershot bite. It also contributes to the appearance of a blunter muzzle as the lower jaw shifts forward. What's acceptable in a breed standard and what is truly healthy for the breed are sometimes in disagreement. Poor bites can affect the overall health of the dog and cause pain and discomfort.

Undershot Bite (Mandibular Prognathism)

An undershot or underbite occurs when the lower jaw protrudes beyond the upper jaw (maxilla) causing the lower incisors to overlap the top and total misalignment of all the teeth. Underbites have similar problems as the level bite, but to a more extreme way including pain.

Overshot Bite

The overbite (mandibular brachygnathism), commonly called "parrot mouth," occurs when the upper jaw (maxilla) is longer than the lower jaw (mandible). This conformation fault positions the lower premolars and molars behind the normal point, ultimately affecting the dog's overall health and condition. An overbite makes it difficult for puppies to suck and chew and for adult dogs to efficiently and comfortably chew and leaves the upper teeth more exposed to trauma. It can also cause considerable pain when the lower incisors hit the palate.

During the growth phase the mouth may become "slightly" overshot until the mandible catches up to the maxilla. When this occurs in a puppy (at approximately five or six months) that previously exhibited in normal scissors bite it is more than likely a temporary condition.

Broken Teeth

Broken teeth or those missing by accident are not penalized because a mechanical injury of this nature cannot be passed on to succeeding generations.

Missing or Extra Teeth

Missing premolars are a problem for the most obvious reasons: chewing. Extra premolars can be a problem if they cause crowding in the mouth. Extra premolars are genetically linked to missing teeth. Both standards call for a full complement (42) of teeth but allow and do not penalize teeth that are broken or missing by accident.

Wry Bite and Other Abnormalities

Wry bite is a lay term for an asymmetrical bite. One side of the jaw grows longer than the other. ASCA disqualifies wry bites. Anything other than a normal occlusion (bite) is detrimental to the breed because it impedes the dog's ability to function without risk of injury.

Any rotation of the teeth indicates the tooth is not seated properly on the jawbone. Base narrow canines are a condition where the lower canine teeth are angled straight upward, instead of tipping outward. Base narrow canines are more common in narrow, more refined heads.

Test Your Judging I.Q. Teeth

1. The relative position of the upper and lower teeth when the jaws are closed is/are the:

　a. Teeth.
　b. Bite.

2. The normal, most correct bite for the Australian Shepherd is a full complement of strong white teeth that meet in a:

　a. Level bite.
　b. Scissors bite.
　c. Overshot bite.
　d. Wry mouth.

3. What is a full complement of teeth?

　a. 42 teeth.
　b. 24 teeth.
　c. 38 teeth.
　d. 44 teeth.

4. ☐ True ☐ False. The right and left sides of the skull should be on the same vertical plane (in a straight line).

5. ☐ True ☐ False. A wry bite is a minor fault.

6. What bite anomaly occurs when the midlines of the upper and lower jaw are <u>not</u> in vertical alignment?

　a. Overshot (longer upper jaw).
　b. Wry mouth.
　c. Undershot (longer lower jaw).

7. When the lower jaw is shorter than the upper jaw it is referred to as a:

　a. Scissors bite.
　b. Level bite.
　c. Undershot bite

d. Overshot bite

8. When the lower teeth protrude in front of the upper jaw teeth it is referred to as a:

   a. Scissors bite.
   b. Wry bite.
   c. Undershot bite.
   d. Overshot bite.

9. ☐ True ☐ False. The level bite, caused by an underdeveloped upper jaw is considered an abnormal occlusion.

10. An undershot bite is listed as a:

   a. Serious fault.
   b. Disqualification.

11. ☐ True ☐ False. An overshot bite greater than 1/8 inch is a serious fault.

12. ☐ True ☐ False. In the correct normal bite, the premolars will line up in a pinking shear arrangement.

13. What is the underlying cause or causes of short central incisors?

   a. An insufficient amount of skeletal support.
   b. Abnormal tooth wear
   c. The central incisors are not well rooted in the jaw bone.
   d. None of the above.

14. ☐ True ☐ False. The scissors bite contributes to the slightly tapered muzzle because the way the jawbone sets into the skull.

Teeth Answers

1-b. Bite.

2-b. Scissors bite.

3-a. 42 teeth are a full complement of teeth.

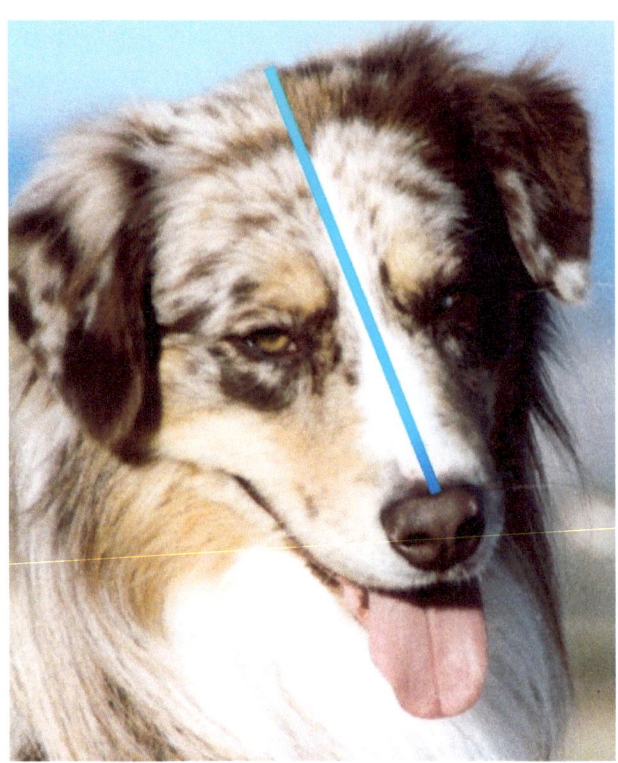

4- True. **"The midline of the head** – starting with the occipital crest (top/back point of the skull), the midpoint between the eyes, the midline of the nose pad and the midline of both the upper and lower arches should lie in a straight line (the same plane). Variation from this alignment of the skull forms the basis of the "wry" bite abnormality." - Donald L. Ross, DVM, MS, Diplomat, ACVD.

5- False. The wry bite is a disqualification in ASCA. The AKC standard doesn't list it as a DQ but states the bite should meet in a scissors bite or level bite.

6-b. Wry mouth.

7-d. An overshot bite, a class 2 prognathism or mandibular brachygnathism.

8-c. An undershot bite (a class 3 mandibular prognathism).

9- True. According the American Veterinary Dental Association (AVDA) the level bite is a class 2 mandibular prognathism and considered an abnormal occlusion.

10-b. The undershot bite is listed a disqualification in both AKC and ASCA breed standards.

11-False. An overshot bite is a disqualification in the ASCA breed standard. The AKC standard allows up to 1/8 of an inch before it's disqualified.

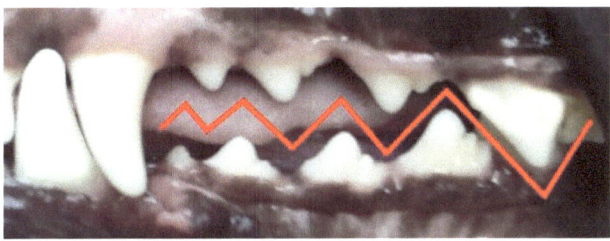

12-True. See the above illustration.

13-a and c. Insufficient skeletal support underlying the central incisors. In other words, the central incisors are not well rooted in the jaw bone, therefore more vulnerable to trauma.

When one or more of the lower incisors are positioned in front of the upper incisors it's referred to as a *Rostral crossbite*, not an undershot bite because the relationship of the upper and lower jaw is normal and the canine and premolar teeth on both sides of the mouth are normally aligned in rostral crossbites.

14-True. The scissors bite results from the set of the jaw-bone and contributes to the underlying structure of a slightly tapered muzzle as pictured above.

 # Eyes

 # Eyes

Expression – Showing attentiveness and intelligence, alert and eager. Gaze should be keen but friendly.

Eyes are brown, blue, amber or any variation or combination thereof, including flecks and marbling. Almond shaped, not protruding nor sunken.

The blue merles and blacks have black pigmentation on eye rims. The red merles and reds have liver (brown) pigmentation on eye rims.

The eyes are very expressive, showing attentiveness and intelligence. They are clear, almond shaped, of moderate size, and set a little obliquely, neither prominent nor sunken. The pupils are dark, well defined, and perfectly positioned. Eye color is brown, blue, amber; or any variation or combination, including flecks and marbling. All eye colors are acceptable in combination with all coat colors.

Faults: Any deviation from almond-shaped eyes.

Expression – Showing attentiveness and intelligence, alert and eager.

It is often said that the eyes are the window into the soul. Eyes should be clear, free from cloudiness, which can indicate impaired vision or blindness.

The normal and most functional structure for the eye opening between the eyelids is almond shaped. Almond shaped eyes are elongated, not round. They are set a little obliquely with well-defined dark pupils.

The almond shaped eyelids shield the eyes from dust and wind and other elements because less of the eyeball is exposed. The external shape of the eye is created by the tissue surrounding the eye rather than the eyeball itself, which is round. The correct head structure dictates and allows the eye to be set obliquely. The elongated opening is created by the relationship bones beneath the eye (the zygomatic arch) and the frontal bone, which forms the forehead, inner casing, and upper portion of each orbit (thereby adding protection from above).

The Australian Shepherd depends upon a moderately curved zygomatic arch, which influences the slightly oblique eye set characteristic of the breed. This allows better protection — deflect a kick — from flying hooves, without creating a restricted visual field.

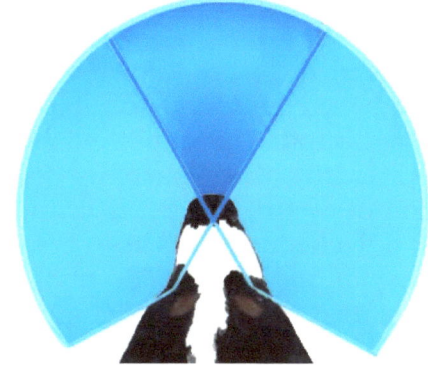

Due the lateral placement of their eyes, Aussies have more peripheral vision than humans or dogs with more frontally positioned eyes.

The wider angle allows them to take in a larger overall picture (sheep in a pasture), but their ability to see close up (binocular overlap) is not as highly developed as a human's. That's why it's easier for Aussies to catch an object moving sideways than one that is hurled straight at its nose.

Faults of round, bulging, and sunken, small eyes result from an incorrect head shape and an inappropriate orbital angle. Consequently, there's a greater chance of serious trauma to the eyes. Haws, the third eyelid located on the inside corner of the eye, are supposed to fit tightly to protect the eye from foreign objects. They are **not** supposed to be visible as pictured above. Prominent haws leave the eye vulnerable to injury. A blow to the head by a hoof or horn can damage the eye, eyelids, and muscles or bones surrounding the eyeball.

Certain eye defects are known to occur in the breed. One clue visible to the naked eye is an offset pupil. The pupil should not be confused with the marbling (mottled) coloration of the iris, which is a trait of the merle and flecked patterns seen throughout the variety of body color. The pupil should be well defined by its positioning and dark color.

Eye color offers variety, contributing to the individuality of the breed as a whole. The eyes may be in any combination of blue, brown, and /or amber, depending on coat color. Eye color is influenced by the inherited coat color and pigmentation. Never give precedence to one eye color or combination. Often, the preference of one eye color over another is generally due to familiarity with one color and lack of familiarity with another.

Test Your Judging I.Q.
Eyes

1. ☐ True ☐ False. The eyes may be almond shaped or roundish.

2. What does set a little obliquely mean?

  a. The outer corners of the eyes are lower than the inner ones
  b. The outer corners of the eyes are higher than the inner ones.

3. ☐ AKC or ☐ ASCA. Which standard describes the eyes as very expressive, showing attentiveness and intelligence?

4. ☐ AKC or ☐ ASCA. "Gaze should be keen, but friendly."

5. ☐ AKC or ☐ ASCA. Which standard specifies the eyes are clear?

6. ☐ AKC or ☐ ASCA. Which standard describes almond shaped, of moderate size, and set a little obliquely?

7. ☐ AKC or ☐ ASCA. Which standard describes the eyes as almond shaped, neither protruding nor sunken?

8. ☐ AKC or ☐ ASCA. Which standard states, "The pupils are dark, well defined, and perfectly positioned?

9. Why does the ASCA standard state, "The pupils are dark, well defined, and perfectly positioned?

  a. A round and centered pupil is the only acceptable shape.
  b. To differentiate between the pupil and Iris.
  c. Eye defects are known to occur within the breed.
  d. All the above.

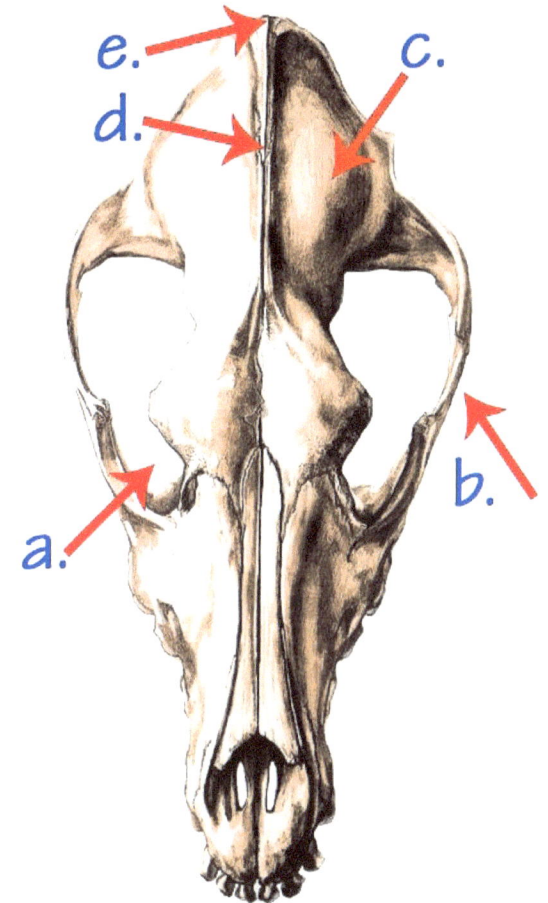

10. Match the above parts of the skull:

a.   Sagittal crest.
b.   Zygomatic arch.
c.   Occiput.
d.   Cranium.
e.   Orbit.

11. What causes the eyes to be positioned more frontal?

a. When the zygomatic arch has less curvature.
b. When the zygomatic arch has more curvature.

12. The eyes are:

a. faulted if they do not contain flecks or marbling.
b. brown, blue or amber or any variation or combination thereof.
c. faulted if both eyes aren't the same color.

13. ☐ True ☐ False. The more curved the zygomatic arch, the more obliquely the eyes are set on the side of the head.

14. Which eye color is preferred in the ASCA standard?

a. Blue.
b. Brown.
c. Amber.
d. One eye of each color.
e. Marbled eyes (multi-colored).
f. None of the above.

15. Red Aussies may have

a. Amber eyes.
b. Brown eyes.
c. Blue eyes.
d. Multi-colored.
e. Two different colored eyes.
f. All of the above.

16. Marbling and flecked patterns of the iris are a:

a. Fault.
b. Severe fault.
c. Disqualification.
d. None of the above.

17. Round, bulging and sunken, or small eyes result from incorrect skeletal features or head shapes. They are a:

a. Fault.
b. Severe fault.
c. Disqualification.
d. None of the above.

18. The Aussie's characteristic almond shape is created by:

a. Eyeball.
b. Bones beneath the eye.
c. Zygomatic arch.
d. Eyelids.
e. b, c, and d.

19. ☐ True ☐ False. Heterochromia is an eye defect of the iris.

Eyes Answers

1-False. Both AKC and ASCA standards call for almond shaped eyes.

2-b. The outer corners are higher than the inner ones.

3-ASCA. The ASCA standard describes the eyes as very expressive showing attentiveness and intelligence.

AKC describes the expression: Showing attentiveness and intelligence, alert and eager.

4-AKC. Gaze should be keen but friendly.

5-ASCA. AKC doesn't specify whether or not the eyes are clear.

6-ASCA. Almond shaped, of moderate size, and set a little obliquely.

7-AKC. Almond shaped, neither protruding nor sunken. ASCA states neither prominent nor sunken.

8-ASCA. AKC doesn't specify anything about the pupils. The pupil is not to be confused with the marbling or (mottled) coloration of the iris, a trait of flecked patterns in merle Aussies.

9-a. The pupils are dark, well defined, and perfectly positioned apart from the iris.

Cloudy eyes may be due to cataracts, and other eye disorders. Iris coloboma is an eye defect found in this breed, particularly in merles. It's often seen as a notched or missing section of the iris. If near the pupil, it will give the pupil a keyhole or oblong shape. A perfectly round, centered pupil is the only acceptable shape.

10-
 a-Orbit.
 b-Zygomatic arch.
 c-Cranium.
 d-Sagittal crest.
 e-Occiput.

11-b. When the zygomatic arch has more curvature, the eyes will be positioned more frontally.

12-b. May be brown, blue or amber, or any variation or combination, including flecks and marbling.

13-False. The flatter the zygomatic arch, the more obliquely the eyes are set on the side of the head.

14-f. None of the above. The eyes may be in any combination of blue, brown, and/or amber. Due to the Aussies unique coloration known as heterochromia.

15-f. All of the above.

16-d. None of the above. Marbling and flecked patterns of the iris are traits of the merle body color. The pupil should not be confused with the multi-coloration of the iris (heterochromia).

17-a. Round, bulging and sunken, small eyes are faulted according to the degree of deviation from the correct almond shape. Faults such as bulging (protruding) eyes can predispose the individual to serious eye trauma.

18-e.

19-False. Heterochromia is a trait of the merle gene causing different-colored eyes.

Notes

Notes

 ## Ears

Ears are triangular, of moderate size and leather, set high on the head. At full attention they break forward and over, or to the side as a rose ear. Prick ears and hanging ears are *severe faults*.

 ## Ears

The ears are set high on the side of the head, are triangular, of moderate size and slightly rounded at the tip. The tip of the ear reaches to, but not further than, the inside corner of the nearest eye. At full attention, the ears should lift from one-quarter (1/4) to one-half (1/2) above the base and break forward or slightly to the side.

Severe Faults:

Prick ears; overly large ears; low set ears with no lift from the base.

Ears are set high on the side of the head and break slightly to the side. They are moderate size and slightly rounded at the tip.

The length of the ear is measured by gently bringing the tip of the ear towards the inside corner of the nearest eye. The tip should not extend past the inside corner of the eye.

Medium sized ears are functionally important to stockdogs that are working in variations of weather throughout the west. The medium sized ear helps dissipate heat for Aussies working in hot weather yet not so large it is unable to reduce the risk of frostbite in frigid weather. The Annotations to the original ASCA Breed Standard stated, "The means of measuring the ear is included to give clarity to the term *moderate size.* Ears breaking from one quarter to a half above the base are ideal, imparting more typical Aussie character. As ears approach three-quarters erect, they more closely resemble the tulip ear of the Collie which is not characteristic of the Aussie."

At full attention, the ears should lift from one-quarter (1/4) to one-half (1/2) above the base. It's considered ideal, imparting more typical Aussie character.

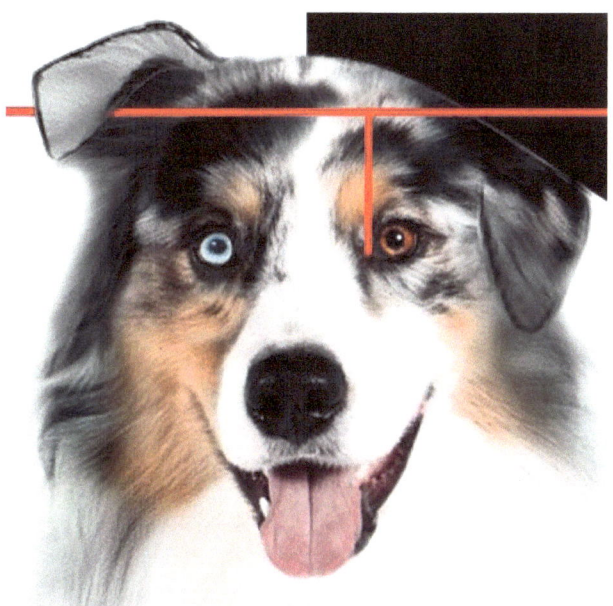

The left ear (above) is correct. The right ear is set (attached at the base) too low on the side of the head. Low ears with no lift or rise in the ear leather are severely faulted because they are untypical of the breed. These are not disqualified because of the relative unimportance of ear set compared to health and structural soundness.

It's not unusual for an individual to have two different types of carriage. This is not a fault, but part of its unique expression.

The inclusion of the term "rose ear" (in the AKC Breed Standard) is misleading. According to the *Complete Dog Book*, an ear shape which resembles a rose is "a small drop ear which folds over and back so as to reveal the burr. The burr is the inside of the ear, i.e., the irregular formation visible within the cup." The naturally occurring ear of the Australian Shepherd can be small and folded over, or the upper front edges can be folded and curved outward. They should not fold over and backward (caused the ear cartilage wrinkling inward at the rear portion), nor should they reveal the burr, as occurs naturally in breeds like the Pug, Whippet, or English Bulldog.

Upright and prick ears are a naturally occurring characteristic in the Australian Shepherd. It's a genetic composition of the breed tracing back to outstanding foundation dogs such as Smedra's Blue Mistingo, Mansker's Freckles, and Wood's Dandy, to name a few. While this trait deviates from desired breed character, it does not affect soundness, nor does it detract from the Australian Shepherd's ability to perform as a stockdog or companion.

Aussie's ears, whatever their shape, rotate independently to catch and amplify sounds. The ears are also important indicators of emotional responses. If ears are taped or surgically altered to break over, a practice known to occur in the show world, the individual is often unable to lift them for directional movement and properly communicate with other dogs and people. It's unfair to the dog.

Test Your Judging I.Q.
Ears

1. Which of the following is **not** a fault?

    a. Prick ears.
    b. Ears that break slightly to the side.
    c. Low set ears with no lift from the base.
    d. Hanging ears.
    e. Moderate size, set on approximate level with eyes.

2. ☐ AKC or ☐ ASCA. At full attention the ears break forward or slightly to the side.

3. ☐ AKC or ☐ ASCA. At full attention the ears break forward and over, or to the side as a rose ear.

4. What does, "The tip of the ear reaches to, but not further than, the inside corner of the nearest eye." mean:

    a. The tip of the ear must **not** extend past the inside corner of the nearest eye.
    b. The tip of the ear must be long enough to reach the inside corner of the nearest eye.

5. ☐ AKC or ☐ ASCA. Which standard states the ears should be set or placed high on side of head?

6. ☐ AKC or ☐ ASCA. Ears are set high on the head?

7. Prick ears are considered:

    a. Severe fault.
    b. Slight fault.
    c. Acceptable.
    d. Faulted to the degree of deviation.
    e. Disqualified.

Ears Answers

1-b. Ears that break to the side.

2-ASCA. At full attention, the ears should lift from one-quarter (1/4) to one-half (1/2) above the base and break forward or slightly to the side.

3-AKC. The definition of rose ear is a small drop ear that folds over and back so as to reveal the burr.

4-a. The tip of the ear must **not** go beyond the inside corner of the nearest eye, but it was not meant the ears had to reach the inside corner of the nearest eye. When the ASCA standard was written the means of measuring the ear was included to give clarity to the term *moderate size*.

Smaller, more moderate ears are not the problem, but ears placed in a lower position on the skull and longer ears are incorrect for the breed.

5-ASCA. Ear set refers to the location they are placed on the head. The base of the ears should be set on or connected high on the side of the head.

6-AKC. The base of the ears should be positioned high on the head.

7-a. While prick ears in the breed's history, they are a considered a severe fault because they detract from desired breed character.

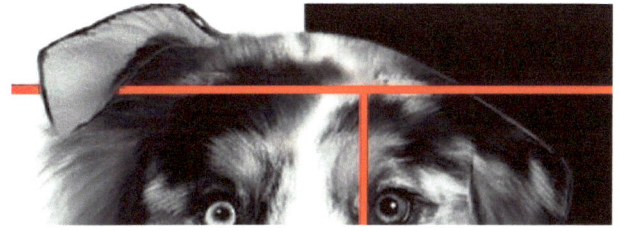

Low set (illustrated above on the right side); overly large ears and hanging ears with no lift from the base are also severely faulted. They are untypical breed traits.

 Neck, Topline and Body

 Neck and Body

Neck is strong, of moderate length, slightly arched at the crest, fitting well into the shoulders. *Topline* – Back is straight and strong, level and firm from withers to hip joints. The croup is moderately sloped. *Chest* is not broad but is deep with the lowest point reaching the elbow. The ribs are well sprung and long, neither barrel chested nor slab-sided. The underline shows a moderate tuck-up. *Tail* is straight, docked or naturally bobbed, not to exceed four inches in length.

The neck is firm, clean, and in proportion to the body. It is of medium length and slightly arched at the crest, setting well into the shoulders. The body is firm and muscular. The topline appears level at a natural four-square stance. The bottom line carries well back with a moderate tuck-up. The chest is deep and strong with ribs well sprung. The loin is strong and broad when viewed from the top. The croup is moderately sloping. The Tail is straight, not to exceed four (4) inches, natural bobtail or docked.

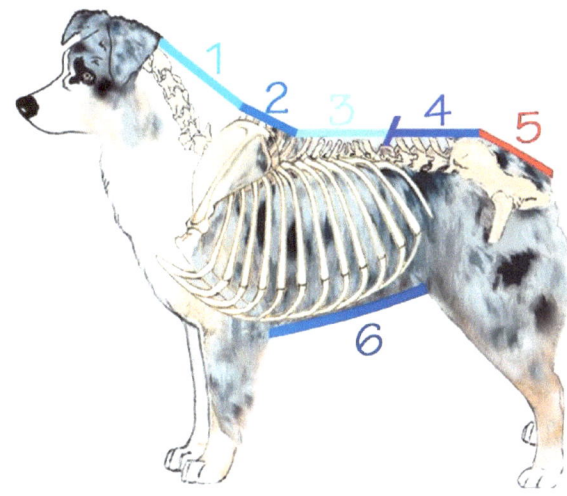

1: neck, 2: the withers, 3: back, 4: loin, 5: croup, and 6: bottom or underline.

The neck is firm and clean which suggests it's free from folds of loose, sagging skin. The skin in Aussies should be close-fitting.

The topline is the "backbone of the operation." The definition of topline, however can be misleading. Topline is often used in the place of backline. The AKC standard calls for the Australian Shepherd to be level from the withers to the hip joints. The hip joint is the ball and socket joint located in the pelvic girdle (under the sloping croup) where the femur is attached. Both standards call for a moderately sloping croup. The slope of the pelvis and associated musculature parallels the slope of the croup made of three sacral vertebrae.

The croup pulls the feet and legs under the body, boosts the center of gravity for fast turns during the initial part of the stride, then sends the power and thrust forward by extending the hind leg in the latter half.

The croup (pelvis) is rotated downward placing the rear legs under the body and therefore under the center of gravity (above).

The head and neck work together as balancing factors. The muscles of the neck tie into the shoulder blades. In the picture (above and below) you can see the neck lifting from the withers to the top of the cervical vertebrae (atlas and axis).

The cervical spine supports the dog's neck and shoulders. The first of seven cervical vertebrae, the atlas, is responsible for the up and down motion of the head on the neck. The second cervical vertebrae, the axis, enables the side-to-side movement of the head on the neck.

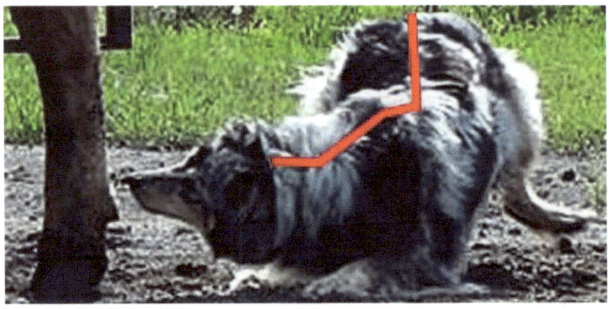

You can see the spine twisting from the white tip of the bobtail all the way to the tip of the nose as the head turns to grip the cow's heel.

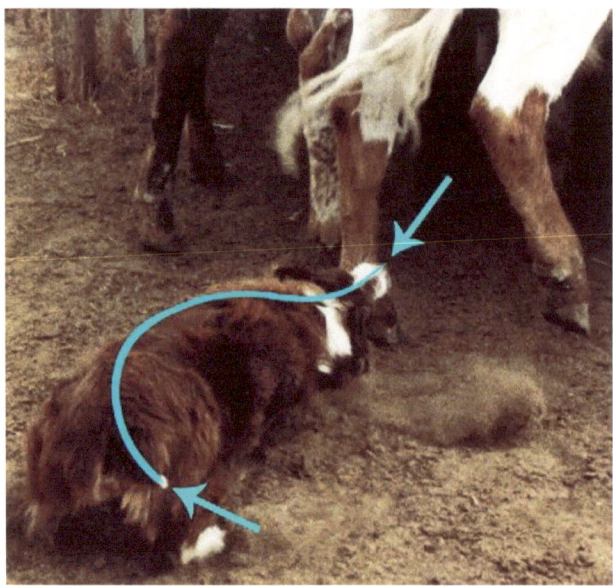

The role played by the head and neck in maneuverability is highly significant in regulating and shifting the center of gravity. By extending the head and neck forward, the Aussie shifts its center of gravity forward, when negotiating turns, its head and neck lift up to draw the center of gravity back as opposed to propelling it forward.

An Aussie scaling the side of an embankment to gather sheep grazing on the steep hillside. The breed's sloping croup that enables it to work sheep in mountain terrain also enables the Australian Shepherd's ability for quick turning. The bobtail is used for balance.

The croup (pelvis) pulling the feet and legs under the body as pictured above. It provides power and thrust when the hind legs are extended.

The loin on working dogs needs to be close-coupled and muscular (broad when viewed from above) because it's not supported by any other bones of the structure. It contains thick, telegraphic muscles that surround seven lumbar vertebrae and transmits the power from the hindquarter to the shock-absorbing forequarter.

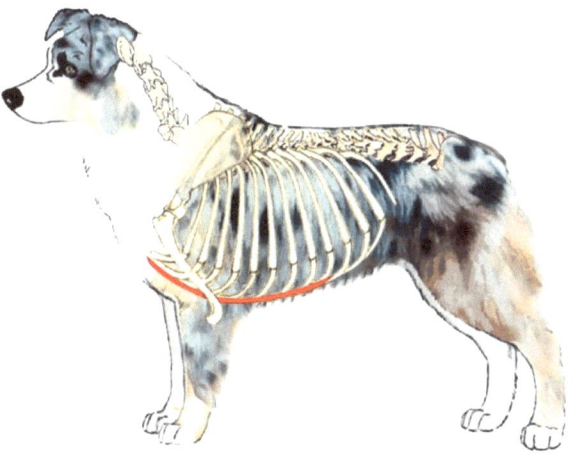

The rib cage and sternum protect the inner organs. It should be broad and long, gently arching outward. Moderate depth, length, and width allows adequate chest expansion for breathing, yet tapers effectively to combat lateral displacement (side to side movement) during locomotion.

The bottom line carries well back with a moderate abdominal tuck-up. The incline of the tuck-up is important because it enables the hind leg assembly to fold underneath the body. It should begin at the 9th rib. If it tucks up too soon or sharply it restricts the internal organs and is referred to as a herring gut.

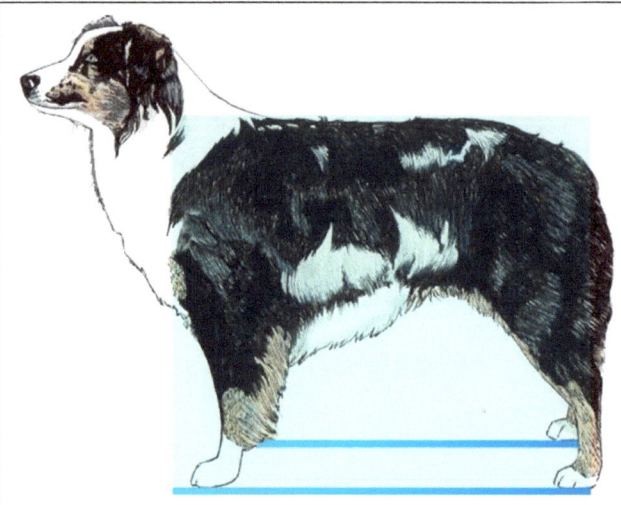

The ASCA Breed Standard Committee included the words, **at a natural four-square stance** because it is the correct, natural stance for the <u>slightly longer than tall</u> Australian Shepherd, and defines how the breed is to be shown, preventing possible faults to be camouflaged with an unnatural stance.

Test Your Judging I.Q. Neck, Topline and Body

1. The most forward projection of the rib cage which forms the front of the forechest is called the:

  a. Brisket.
  b. Sternum.
  c. Manubrium.
  d. Keel.

2. The lower curved outline of the chest / ribcage is called the:

  a. Brisket.
  b. Sternum.
  c. Prosternum.
  d. Keel.

3. ☐ True ☐ False. The sternum is connected to the ribs by cartilage.

4. The shape of the ribcage affects the:

  a. Shoulder layback.
  b. Lung function.
  c. Gait.
  d. Weight distribution.

5. ☐ AKC or ☐ ASCA. Chest is not broad but is deep with the lowest point reaching the elbow.

6. What does rib spring refer to?

  a. Lung and heart room.
  b. Outward curve of the ribs that form the expandable cage beginning at the 5th rib.
  c. Chest cavity that protects the heart and lungs.
  d. All the above.

7. Which is correct shape for the rib cage for the Australian Shepherd?

  a. Round, well arched.
  b. Egg-shaped.
  c. Flat-ribbed and deep through the brisket.

8. What role does rib spring play on gait?

  a. Helps stamina.
  b. Effects lateral displacement.
  c. Aids or hinders convergence.
  d. Agility.
  e. None of the above.

9. When an Aussie toes-out, it's because:

  a. Lack of maturity.
  b. Lacks rib spring.
  c. Tied at elbows.
  d. Tied at shoulders.
  e. Any of the above.

10. What type of movement results when a dog elbows-in?

  a. Paddling.
  b. Padding.
  c. Hackney gait.

11. ☐ True ☐ False. Australian Shepherds have 19 pairs of ribs.

12. ☐ True ☐ False. The back is made up of 20 thoracic vertebrae (above).

13. Where does the Aussie's back end?

    a. 1st lumbar vertebrae.
    b. 13th thoracic vertebrae.
    c. Point of hip (Ilium).
    d. Sacrum vertebrae.
    e. Tail.

14. The neck should be:

    a. Strong, short, slightly arched at the crest.
    b. Strong, moderate length, slightly arched at the crest.
    c. Strong, long, slightly arched at the crest.

15. The length of the neck is determined:

    a. By shoulder layback.
    b. By the thickness and length of the vertebrae that make up the neck.

16. ☐ True ☐ False. The ewe neck is caused by inverted cervical vertebrae of the neck.

17. The topline is straight and strong and should be:

    a. Slightly arched over the loin.
    b. Soft and flexible from the withers to the hip joints.
    c. Level and firm from the withers to hip joints.
    d. Firm.

18. ☐ True ☐ False. The breed standard states "Back is straight and strong, level and firm from withers to hip joints." A dog that is high at the withers should be disqualified.

19. ☐ True ☐ False. A roach back refers to the arched loin.

20. ☐ True ☐ False. The Aussie uses its head and neck for balance to counteract actions of the hindquarters. They assist in the Aussie's maneuverability.

21. ☐ True ☐ False. The loin's unique shaped vertebrae give it flexibility.

22. A muscular loin in Aussies may present as:

    a. A small arch.
    b. Flat (no arch).

23. The coupling refers to:

    a. Loin.
    b. Length of body.
    c. Croup.
    d. The area from the withers to the tail.

24. ☐ True ☐ False. The topline between the withers and the croup is level.

25. The croup is described in the AKC and ASCA breed standards as:

    a. Level with topline.
    b. Moderately sloping.

26. ☐ True ☐ False. The tail set should appear level with the back.

27. ☐ True ☐ False. Australian Shepherds are born with naturally long tails that are docked at birth.

28. What is a herring gut?

    a. The bottom line tucks up gradually.
    b. The bottom line tucks up abruptly.

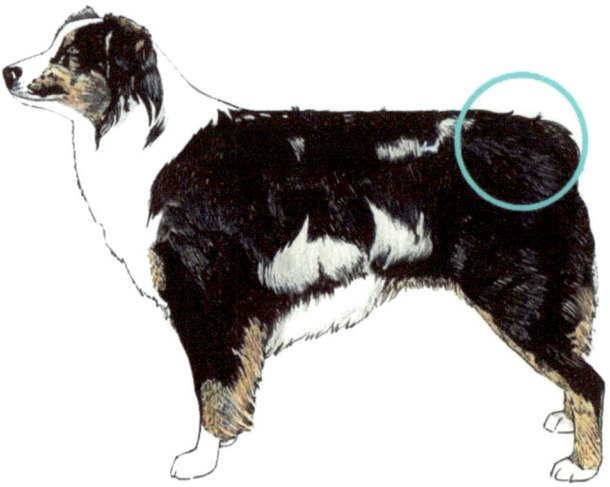

29. ☐ Sprinter or ☐ Trotter?

30. ☐ Sprinting drivetrain or ☐ Trotting drivetrain?

31. ☐ Top ☐ Bottom. Which stance is more correct for the breed?

Neck, Topline and Body Answers

1-c. Manubrium of sternum also referred to as the prosternum.

2-b (a, b or d). Sternum also known as keel or brisket.

3-True. The first seven ribs connect directly to the sternum with costal cartilage that helps the chest cavity expand for breathing.

4-b and c. Lung function. Any deformity of the chest and ribs can cause a smaller place for the lungs to expand. The shape of the ribcage can also affect the dog's gait. Why? Because it directly impacts placement of the upper arm and elbow.

5-AKC.

6-b. Rib spring refers to the outward curvature of the ribs that form the expandable cage. The top of the ribs come out of the thirteen thoracic vertebrae beginning at the fifth rib.

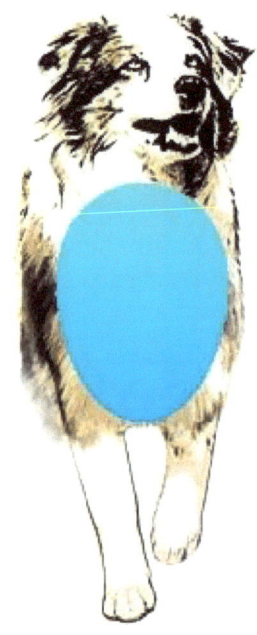

7-b. An egg-shaped oval is the correct rib spring for Australian Shepherds. It's tapered down. It allows adequate lung room without hindering the front legs ability to converge as necessary. A round rib cage, a barrel chest, would cause the Aussie to elbow-out and reduce stamina.

8-b, c and d. Rib spring helps or hinders the dog's ability to converge (draw its paws beneath the center of gravity) to minimize lateral displacement (side-to-side motion). Agility is also dependent on convergence, which enables each Aussie to swivel (pivot) from the center line of the body, rather than pulling itself around.

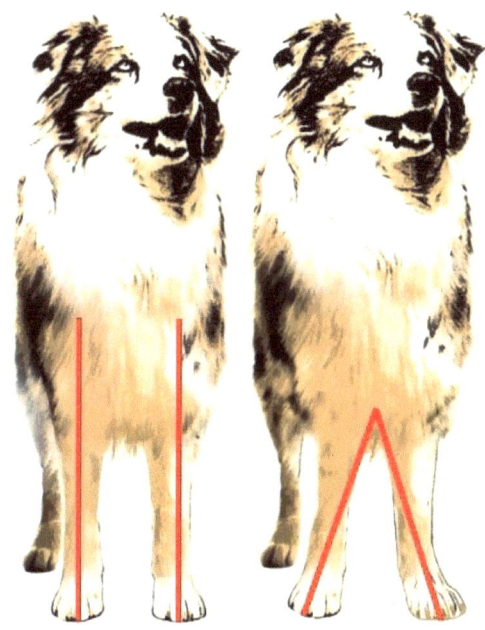

9-d. Any of the above. The dog's forelegs should drop vertical (left) to the ground, not outward forming a triangle as pictured on the right. There are various reasons for a dog to toe-out. Toeing out in a young dog can be due to inadequate rib spring through lack of maturity. The depth of ribs will not change, but as the young dog develops, the ribs will widen outward causing the elbows to line up correctly. Slab-sided or flat ribs can also cause the toes to point "east-west." Slab sided also limits room for lung expansion.

The origin of "toeing out" in some dogs is a weakness in the pastern joint, not at the elbows which will not improve with maturity.

10-a. When a dog is tied at the elbow its feet will flip out in a paddling motion.

11-False. All dogs have 13 pairs of ribs. 12 pairs that connect to the sternum and one pair called floating ribs.

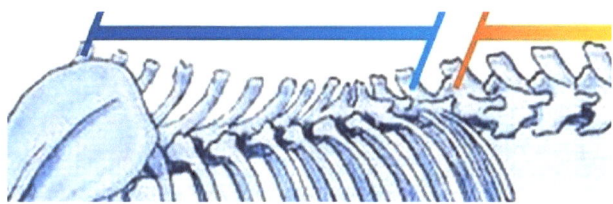

12-False. The back is made up of 13 thoracic vertebrae that supports the chest and abdominal region (blue to blue). The latter half of the spine is made of seven lumbar vertebrae (orange) that supports the dog's lower back and hindquarters.

13-b. The back ends at the last or 13th thoracic vertebrae. The loin begins at the 1st lumbar vertebrae.

14-b. The neck should be strong, moderate in length, and slightly arched at the crest.

15-b. Length of neck is determined by the thickness and length of the vertebrae that make up the neck.

16-False. The ewe neck is caused by a straight line of vertebrae rather than the correct, naturally arched vertebrae due to a weak cervical ligament and muscling.

17-c. According to the standard, level and firm from the withers to hip joints. When viewed from the side the dog's **backline** should be strong and appear level between the shoulders and the loin. The topline includes the sloping croup. Knowledgeable judges understand the muscles may be slightly arched over the loin when Aussies are in working condition. This is from muscular development, not a curved spine.

18-False. Anatomically speaking the withers are often a little higer than the rest of the back because of the nature of the thoracic vertebrae.

19-False. Roach back refers to the convex curvature of thoracic vertebrae of the back, not the lumbar vertebrae of the loin. A slight rise over the loin due to muscular development should never be confused with a roached (arched back). The back should be level and firm.

20-True. Additionally, the shoulder muscles are attached to the neck which is why the neck lifts out of the shoulders.

21-False. The loin is flexible because the absence of ribs. It's where the body tucks up when the dog sprints or is moving into or out of position to heel a cow or evade an attack. The healthy lumbar region is necessary for agility.

22-a. Small arch. The lumbar region may be slightly arched through muscular development.

23-a. The loin (coupling). The area from the ribs to the pelvis. Close-coupled refers to a short length.

24-False. The backline is level, BUT the croup slopes.

25-b. Moderately sloping.

26-False. Handlers often trim the croup to make the tail appear level with the back, but Australian Shepherds should have a moderately sloping croup. Therefore, the tail set is slightly lower than the topline.

27-False. Aussies are born with varying tail lengths from short natural bobtails to full length. Both Australian Shepherd standards allow tails to be surgially docked not to exceed four inches in length. Tails that exceed the four-inch allowance are penalized to the extent of the deviation. In countries where tail docking bans exist an Australian Shepherd being shown with a tail longer than 4 inches shall not be faulted and/or penalized.

28-b. A herring gut tucks up abruptly which restricts lung and heart function.

29-Trotter. The croup of the trotter is flatter than the sprinter. An Aussie with a high set tail has a fairly flat croup. Note: There's a difference between tail set and tail carriage.

30-Sprinting drivetrain. The croup of the sprinter is more heavily musceld, joined to a steeper, longer pelvis. The longer pelvis and croup allows more area for the type of muscling necessary for quickness.

The sprinting drivetrain delivers speed to turn back runaways and also provides the specific action of the hock and stifle needed to low-heel cows.

31-The dog on the top. Why? When a dog is built correctly for function, base of support is under the center of gravity. Consequently, the "four-square" stance is the most natural, correct stance for the breed.

Notes

Notes

 ## Forequarters

 ## Forequarters

Shoulders – Shoulder blades are long, flat, fairly close set at the withers and well laid back. The upper arm, which should be relatively the same length as the shoulder blade, attaches at an approximate right angle to the shoulder line with forelegs dropping straight, perpendicular to the ground. *Legs* straight and strong. Bone is strong, oval rather than round. *Pastern* is medium length and very slightly sloped. Front dewclaws may be removed. *Feet* are oval, compact with close knit, well arched toes. Pads are thick and resilient.

The shoulder blades (scapula) are well laid back, with the upper arm (humerus) slightly longer than the shoulder blade. Both the upper arm and shoulder blade are well muscled. The forelegs are straight and strong, perpendicular to the ground, with moderate bone. The point of the elbow is set under the withers and is equidistant from the withers to the ground. Pasterns are short, thick, and strong, but still flexible, showing a slight angle when viewed from the side. Feet are oval shaped, compact, with close knit, well-arched toes. Pads are thick and resilient; nails short and strong. Dewclaws may be removed.

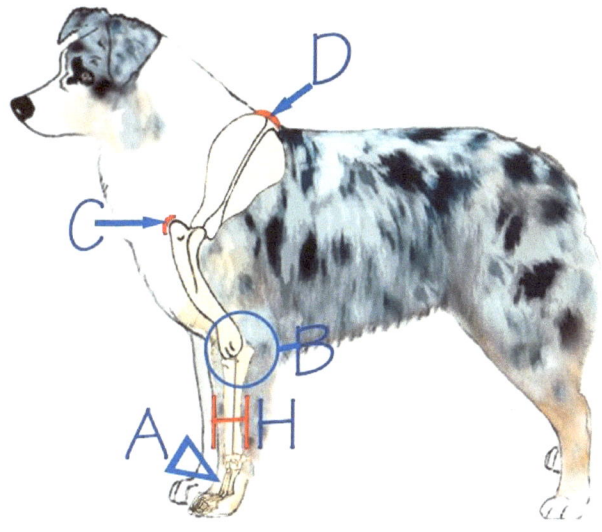

A. Pasterns
B. Elbow joint
C. Point of shoulder
D. Point of withers
H. Radius and ulna (Forearm)

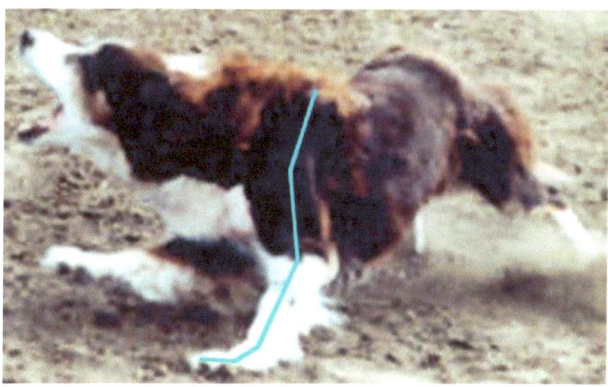

The front assembly is the mechanism for steering and braking. It serves to stabilize and oppose lateral displacement, make turns, control and lift the center of gravity.

The front assembly supports at least 60 percent of the dog's entire body weight standing still. During a stride it absorbs the impact when the movement (trotting running or jumping) is completed.

The scapula (shoulder blade) is often referred to as the cornerstone of the front assembly. The ball-and-socket joint of the scapula is attached to the skeleton by fibrous connective tissue (unlike the ball-and-socket of the pelvis, which is linked to the spine by the sacroiliac joint).

Muscles stabilize and support the scapula. They pull the scapula forward and around on the rib (thoracic) cage. The also limit flexion and extension and enable the shoulder to open sufficiently to assist lateral extension of the leg as pictured below.

The pivot point is located at the upper middle of the scapula where it is attached to the body, which is also the weight bearing point for the front assembly.

As the shoulder rotates forward, the muscles and connective tissues increase reach.

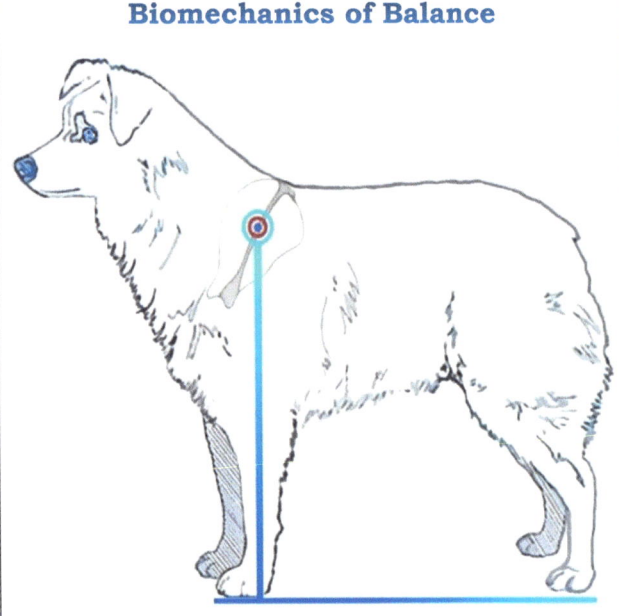

Biomechanics of Balance

For static, standing balance, the legs need to drop with a column of support beneath the weight bearing point of the front assembly. The slight angle of the pastern places the weight of the animal on the metacarpal (palmar) pad. The foot is more likely to break down when the majority of weight is carried on toes rather than the metacarpal pad and then distributed to the forward supporting digital pads.

The front-to-back sloping of the shoulder blade is referred to as layback. This terminology is rooted in the equine world where well-laid-back shoulders are desirable for a smooth riding horse. While there are many comparisons that can be made between the anatomy of horses and dogs, there is one significant difference. Dogs have flexible backs and are not ridden.

Aussies made for sustained trotting have more shoulder layback and a little more slope to the front pastern than their sprinting cousins. Aussies built for agility have slightly steeper shoulders (less slope) and a slightly shorter upper arm. There is also less slope to the pasterns. To be absolutely clear, we are **not** talking about straight angulation like the Chinese Shar-Pei or Chow Chow breeds that are not built to execute a 180-degree rollback at a sprint.

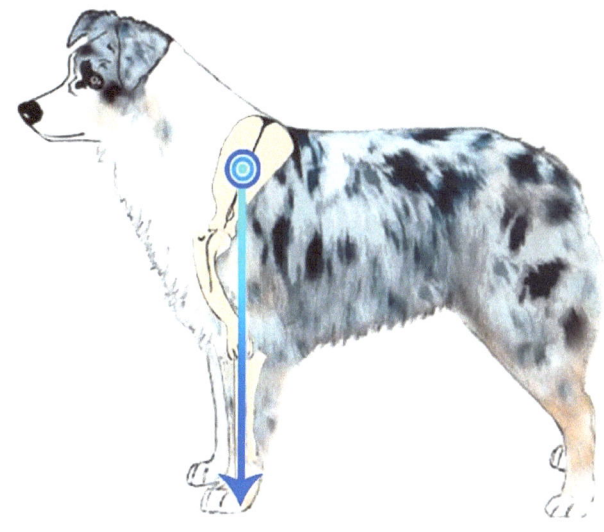

To get a rough idea of the dog's shoulder angulation or layback, it's necessary for the front legs to be vertical to the ground. Ideally, you should be able to drop a plumb line from the reciprocating center (midpoint) of the shoulder through the vertical line of support, the bones of the forearm to the metacarpal pad.

A young cowdog (above) in a natural stance. The upper arm is seemingly shorter than the shoulder blade. The front assembly is balanced by a reciprocating hind assembly. The same dog (below) moving confidently towards a heifer with ideal flexion and stabilization from the shoulders.

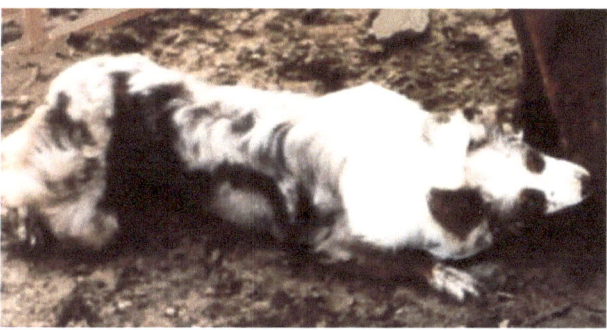

It's not uncommon to find Aussies with a slightly shorter upper arm. The benefit of a more moderate front assembly is the dog's ability to drop to the ground and position themselves to low-heel cattle or dodge flying hooves to avoid a kick.

The shoulders are not fixed or immobile but pulled forward and backwards by muscles for a full range of motion to reach forward, rotate back and assist with balance.

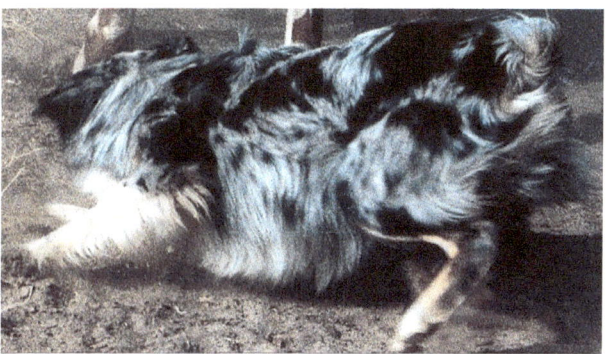

The same dog low-heeling the heifer (above) to illustrate the moderate stifle in action.

The front pasterns connect the radius and ulna to the feet. They work in conjunction with the feet to provide lift to the front assembly and flex to absorb external forces when the foot meets the ground. This in turn minimizes the stress to the bones that form the toes. Pasterns are made up of five metacarpal bones that originate at the knee (carpal bones). They need to be short, thick and strong but flexible enough to reduce concussion when running, jumping, and turning.

The front assembly needs to be coordinated with the hind assembly. In other words, the angulation of the forequarters **must** correspond with the angulation of the hindquarters.

On the Diagonal

The carpal pad located on the inner surface of the front pastern area is important to the functionality of the Aussie. It stabilizes and reduces torque as it touches the ground (above) to maintain balance. It also cushions feet and legs as the dog sprints and makes tight turns.

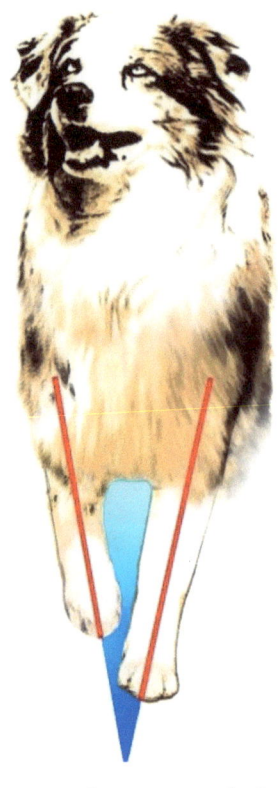

Long, weak or broken-down pasterns do not give adequate support to the rest of the leg. Weak pasterns cause fatigue and predispose the dog to hyperextension and injury of the pasterns and knees at fast speeds.

As the dog is trotting toward the viewer, the feet converge toward the mid point or (line of gravity) under the body. Simply put, the legs from the shoulder to paw, resemble a "V" shape as the dog's legs are drawn underneath in the trotting gait.

As speed increases, both front and rear feet converge toward the centerline of gravity beneath the body. This occurs in the show-ring or in the real world working sheep.

Appropriate length of leg is necessary for Aussies working the rugged terrain on various ranching operations throughout the American west and Canada. Short legs hinder the dog's stamina and ability to work in mud, heavy snow and deep sand.

Feet

You often hear about reach and drive, but what about feet? The feet support the Aussie's entire body weight. The front feet support more than half of the dog's weight. As a result, the front feet are slightly larger (broader) than the hind feet. Therefore, correct, sound feet are essential. Poor feet can limit athletic ability and lead to impaired performance and injury.

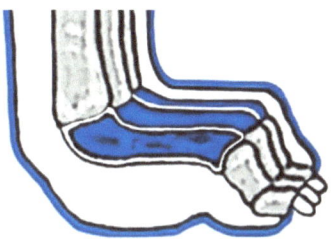

The breed standards state: "Feet are oval shaped." The oval shaped foot described in the breed standard is a semi-hare also known as a modified hare-foot. The oval shaped, **modified hare-foot** is the most functional type of foot for the Australian Shepherd, a breed that needs to be able to trot for certain distances, change directions, stop abruptly or alter gait instantly in rugged terrain. The longer third digital bones are also helpful for the type of quick initial speed needed for outrunning errant livestock.

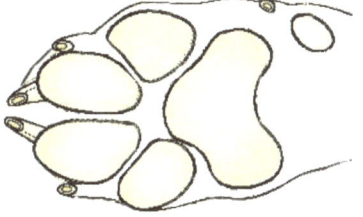

Each foot has four digital pads, the heart-shaped metacarpal pad and a functioning dewclaw to support the foot. The dog's pads aid in traction and shock absorption. Thickness is important for absorbing shock and increased endurance. Resilience aids in flexibility. Traction is necessary for agility enabling quick turns and effective sprinting. Uneven wear on the dog's pads themselves will reveal unbalances in gait. If the metacarpal (palmar) pad is not sharing the weight with the digital pads, then they are carrying an extra burden. This will strain the toes causing early breakdown.

Weak feet (splayed, flat, and broken down) are more easily affected by rough, uneven terrain. Splayed and flat feet are serious faults because they lead to early breakdown and lameness. Splayed feet expose the webbing to injury. What causes feet to splay? The tendons and ligaments that hold the digits together are lax, so the toes spread apart. It's generally an inherited defect but can be caused by an injury. When that happens, it will appear in the injured foot only, not the other feet. Long toenails can increase force placed on the digits (toes) and predispose them to fractures and other injuries.

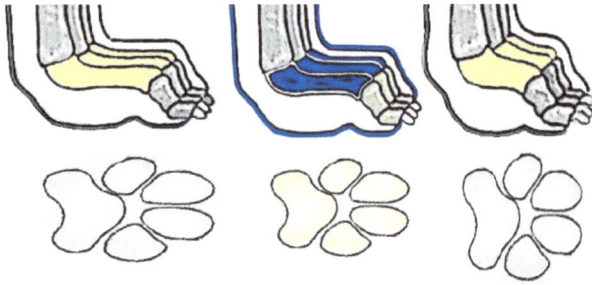

Left to right: Hare foot, oval foot also known as the modified hare-foot, cat-like foot.

The shorter third digital bones resulting in the cat-like foot (a deep, round foot with toes nearer the base of the heel of the foot) may be beneficial for the trotting specialist. It requires less energy to operate (less power to lift); but it lacks adequate leverage necessary for unusual agility (ability to change direction or alter gait instantly), which is a hallmark for our breed. The modified hare-foot appears to be somewhat flatter than the compact, highly arched, cat-like foot; however too often judges confuse the slightly flatter toes of the elongated hare foot with flat and broken-down feet. Flat, broken-down feet lack sufficient padding, and spring. Splayed feet should also be penalized harshly.

The breed standard also states the foot pads should be thick and resilient. Why? The foot pads are where the "rubber meets the road." This padding (thick skin and fatty connective tissue) is important for traction, shock absorption, and protection from rocky surfaces, briars, thorns, frozen ground and ice granules etc. Thick pads also protect their feet from frost bite.

When the four smaller digital pads tip upwards, they expose the webbing to injury similar to the splay foot. The third digital bones aren't adequately supported. This type of conformation is weak causing the foot to break down. **If you have *no foot*, you have *no dog.***

Dogs don't work on stock without risk. They can be kicked, stepped on, run over, butted, rolled, horned, or otherwise injured. It requires quick thinking, athletic ability and sound feet to escape a charging animal. An Aussie without sound feet is not sound and its usefulness is limited.

Test Your Judging I.Q. Forequarters

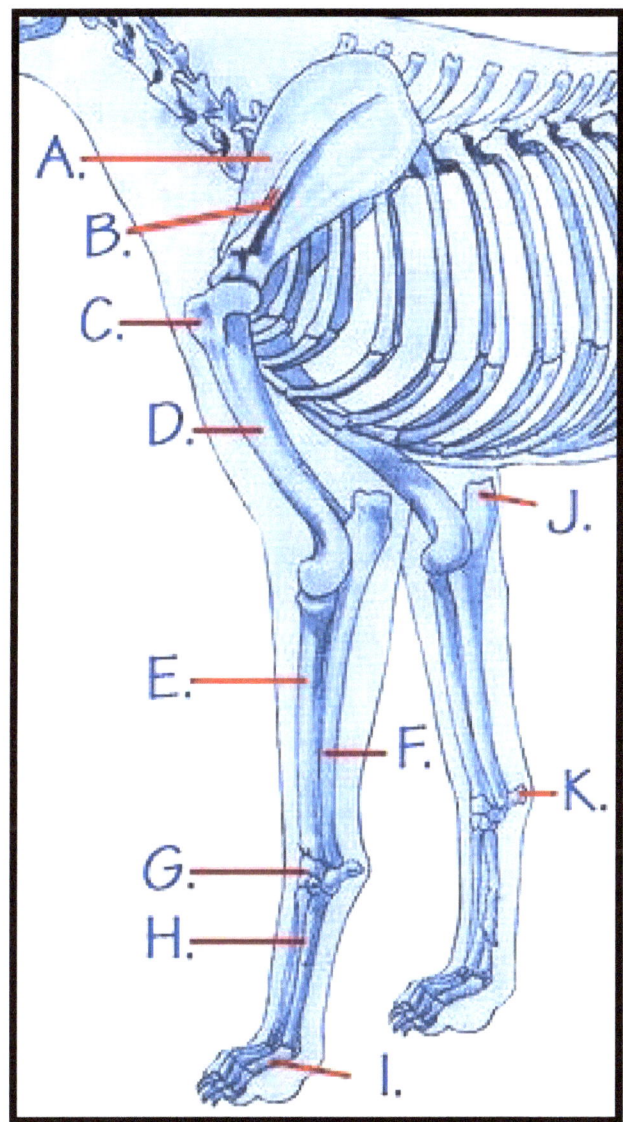

1. Match the above parts:

Scapular spine	
Point of shoulder	
Ulna	
Scapula	
Wrist	
Radius	
Elbow	
Digits	
Humerus	
Pastern	
Carpal pad	

2. Can you list the front limb counterparts to the rear limbs?

2a. Pelvis
- 2a.

2b. Upper Thigh (Femur)
- 2b.

2c. Lower Thigh (Tibia and Fibula)
- 2c.

2d. Rear Pastern / Hock (Metatarsus)
- 2d.

3. ☐ True ☐ False. An Australian Shepherd with large bone is better built to withstand the impact of a cow kick than an Aussie with smaller bone.

4. ☐ True ☐ False. The Australian Shepherd is an endurance trotting breed.

5. ☐ True ☐ False. The shoulder blade and upper arm (Humerus) are attached to the dog by ball and socket joint.

6. The pastern's main function is for:

    a. Weight bearing.
    b. Absorbing shock.
    c. Driving.
    d. Balance.
    e. Connecting the forearm to the foot.

7. ☐ True ☐ False. Pasterns need to be well laid back so they don't lead to fatigue and hyperextension.

8. ☐ True ☐ False. The compact cat-like foot is designed for quick speed and jumping ability.

9. ☐ True ☐ False. The mechanical advantage of the modified-hare foot is quick speed, turns and jumping ability.

10. ☐ True ☐ False. The difference between the cat-like and the modified-hare paw is the length of the third digital bones.

11. ☐ Cat-like foot ☐ Modified-hare foot. Two toes at the center are longer than the outer toes.

12. ☐ Cat-like foot ☐ Modified-hare foot Type of foot that requires less energy to operate, but it lacks necessary spring required for quickness and agility.

13. ☐ Cat-like ☐ Modified-hare foot. Type of foot provides quick speed and jumping ability.

14. The oval shaped foot described in the breed standard is a:

    a. Cat-like foot.
    b. Hare foot.
    c. Modified hare-foot.

15. ☐ True ☐ False. An Aussie with well-laid back angulation is more agile than an Aussie with slightly steeper angulation.

16. The forequarters are designed for:

    a. Support.
    b. Driving.
    c. Catching gravity.

17. ☐ True ☐ False. The radius and ulna operate as separate bones.

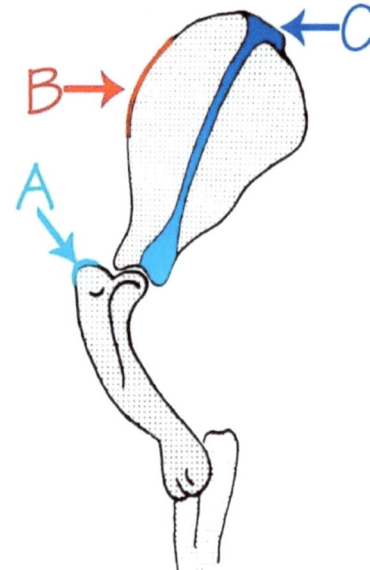

Word Bank

Cervical angle, Crest of scapular spine, Point of shoulder.

18. Use the Word Bank to lable the above diagram.

A- _____

B- _____

C- _____

19. ☐ True ☐ False. The crest of the scapula spine is the place where the shoulder blade flattens.

20. ☐ True ☐ False. A popular method of estimating shoulder angulation is by locating the point of shoulder with one hand and crest of the scapular spine with the other hand.

21. ☐ True ☐ False. The shoulder blade (scapula) is attached by a process of muscle and ligaments which allows for lateral mobility and shock absorption.

22. ☐ True ☐ False. The central (3rd and 4th) digital pads along with the metacarpal pads of the front feet play a significant role in distributing forces during weight bearing and in storing or absorbing mechanical forces in the forequarters.

23. The AKC Breed Standard states the shoulder blades should be:

   a. Short, flat and straight.
   b. Short and upright.
   c. Long and slightly straight.
   d. Long, flat and well-laid back.

24. ☐ True ☐ False. An Australian Shepherd built with the type of shoulder layback that produces a trotting style with maximum reach and drive is more agile than an Aussie with a moderate shoulder assembly (less slope).

25. ☐ True ☐ False. Australian Shepherds have collar bones.

26. The upper arm is the anatomical area:

   a. between the pastern and elbow.
   b. between the shoulder and the elbow.

27. ☐ True ☐ False. Dewclaws on the front legs are a matter of personal preference.

28. What is the correct shoulder layback for the Australian Shepherd's breed function as a working stockdog?

   a. Well-laid back.
   b. Moderately sloping.
   c. 45-degree angle.
   d. None of the above.

29. ☐ True ☐ False. Fiddle front is caused by a slab-sided rib cage.

Word Bank
Correct alignment, Pidgeon toed, Toes-out.

Use the **Word Bank** to write the front limb alignment terminology below:

30. _____

31. _____

63

32. _____

33. ☐ Padding ☐ Paddling. When the front legs swing forward on an outward arc.

34. What causes paddling?

    a. Shoulder blades being too far back on the thorax.
    b. Elbows and/or shoulder joints are restricted.
    c. Immaturity.
    d. All the above.

35. ☐ True ☐ False. The dog's tibia is comparable to the human shin bone.

36. If presented with identical littermates, the only difference is their length of leg measured from ground to the elbow (compared to the distance from the sternum to the withers). Which Aussie has a better advantage to function as a working stockdog handling cattle on the unfenced open range?

  ☐ **a.** Slightly shorter legs ☐ **b.** Slightly longer legs.

Forequarters Answers

1:
A. Scapula (Shoulder blade).
B. Scapular Spine.
C. Point of shoulder.
D. Humerus (Upper arm).
E. Radius.
F. Ulna.
G. Wrist (Carpus / Carpal bones).
H. Pastern (Metacarpals).
I. Digits (Foot).
J. Elbow (Tip of ulna).
K. Carpal pad.

2:
2a-Shoulder Blade.
2b-Upper Arm (Humerus).
2c-Forearm / foreleg (Radius and Ulna).
2d-Front Pastern.

3- False. Research suggests that large bones are more porous than smaller, moderate sized bones (when comparing healthy animals of the same size and age).

4- False. It's a myth. Working Australian Shepherds do NOT mainly trot but are required to use many gaits from a walk to a sprint in the real world.

5- False. The shoulder blade and upper arm are attached by ligaments and muscles unlike the hindquarters which are attached by a ball and joint.

6- b and e.

7- False. Pasterns that are too lax (too much slope) will lead to fatigue, hyperextension and break down.

8- False. The shorter digital bones lack the necessary leverage action required for quick turns and agility. The cat-like foot is designed for effortless, long distance trotting because it takes less energy to lift, thus increasing endurance.

9- True. The longer toes of the hare foot give more leverage for quick speed and agility.

10-True. The two center toes in the hare foot are noticeably longer. They are not as highly arched as the cat-like foot either.

11- Modified-hare foot.

12- Cat-like foot.

13- Modified-hare foot.

14- Modified hare-foot also known as a semi-hare foot.

15-False. Well-laid-back shoulders are designed for the trotting specialist (sustained trotters), not for agility.

16-a and c. By design, the forequarters are designed for support and catching gravity.

17-False. The forearm is made up of the radius and ulna. They are fused together and operate as a single bone but permit the dog to rotate the limb on its axis. The tibia and fibula in the hind assembly operate in the same way.

18:
(A) Point of shoulder.
(B) Cervical angle.
(C) Crest of scapular spine.

19-True.

20-True. The easiest way to estimate shoulder angulation is to use palpable points. Touch the point of shoulder with your left hand. Then glide your right hand over the cervical angle to the highest point of the scapula. **Note:** No matter what type of angulation the shoulder has, it must be balanced by a corresponding hindquarter.

21-True.

22-True. The same principal applies for the rear digital and metatarsal (plantar) pads.

23-d. Long, flat and well-laid back.

24-False. Shoulders that are set well-laid back are designed for sustained trotters.

There is a popular misconception the somewhat steeper shoulder layback is synonymous with pounding and faulty movement. Faulty movement occurs when the forequarters are NOT in balance with hindquarters. When the front and rear assembly is in sync and balanced unto itself, the gait will be coordinated regardless of the angulation of its skeletal members.

The shoulder blades and upper arm of working Australian Shepherds are more conservative, than the well-laid-back shoulder blade on their show-type cousins.

25-False. Dogs do not have collar bones. The shoulder blades do not attach to other bones.

26-b. The upper arm is located between the shoulder and elbow.

27-True. Whether or not an individual has front dewclaws should have no bearing whatsoever on judging in the show ring. People remove front dewclaws for easier grooming or to make the front leg look smoother. Current research indicates that dogs without dewclaws have more foot injuries and are more prone to arthritis.

28-b. Moderately sloping. In other words, lesser angle off the vertical than well-laid back. Correctness has to be defined by function. If we look at the Aussies's job description we discover Australian Shepherds depend on quick bursts of speed to sprint ahead, stop abruptly with a simultaneous rollback to turn back livestock and then drop down low enough to avoid being kicked.

The 45-degree angle is imaginary. It's a myth. It is **nonexistent.** But, if it did exist...it would be incorrect for the Aussie.

29- False. Fiddle front is generally caused by the premature closure of the growth plates which causes the front legs to grow crooked or bowed.

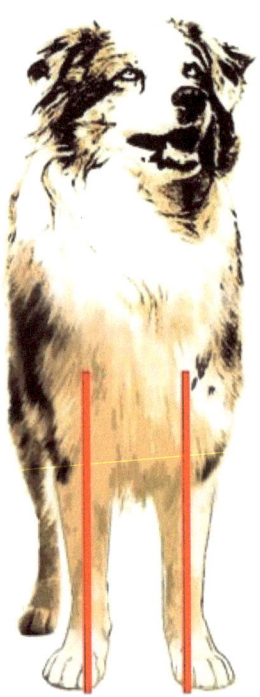

30-Toes-out. The metacarpal bones are aligned outward.

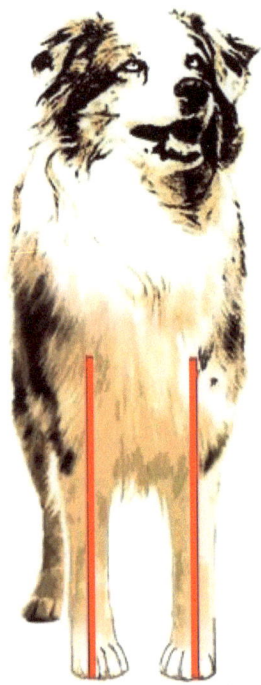

31-Pidgeon toed (Toes-in). The metacarpal bones are aligned inward.

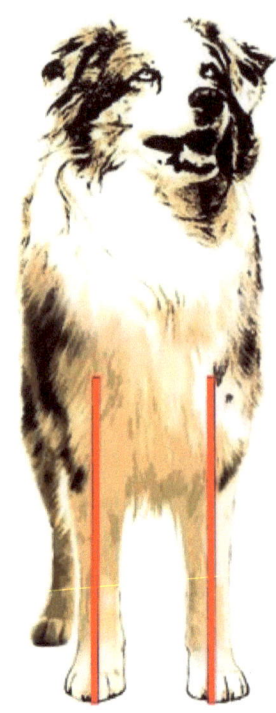

32-Correct alignment. The metacarpal bones are aligned parallel.

33- Paddling also known as *Winging out* occurs when the front feet twist outward as the front legs swing forward. "Winging in" occurs when the dog swings it's foreleg to the inside.

34-d. Paddling is caused when the elbows and/or shoulder joints are restricted initiating the front legs to swing forward on an outward arc also known as tied at the elbows. This may be due to a narrow, immature chest or poor muscle control.

35- True. The canine tibia is similar to our shin bone.

36-b. A little longer length of leg would benefit the individual giving it an advantage to navigate through heavy snow, deep sand, thick mud and tall grass. Short legs hinder stamina as well as the breed's ability to outrun livestock and swim when pushing animals across a body of water. The trend for long bodied, shorter legged dogs reduces athleticism. An Aussie's leg length from the ground to the elbow should be at least equal if not a little longer (but not less than) the distance from the elbow to the withers.

Notes

Notes

 ## Hindquarters

 ## Hindquarters

The width of the hindquarters is equal to the width of the forequarters at the shoulders. The angulation of the pelvis and upper thigh corresponds to the angulation of the shoulder blade and upper arm, forming an approximate right angle. *Stifles* are clearly defined, hock joints moderately bent. The *hocks* are short, perpendicular to the ground and parallel to each other when viewed from the rear. Rear dewclaws must be removed. *Feet* are oval, compact with close knit, well arched toes. Pads are thick and resilient.

Width of hindquarters is approximately equal to the width of the forequarters at the shoulder. The angulation of the pelvis and upper thigh (femur) corresponds to the angulation of the shoulder blade and upper arm. The upper and lower thigh are well muscled. Stifles are clearly defined; hock joints moderately bent. The metatarsi are short, perpendicular to the ground, and parallel to each other when viewed from the rear. Feet are oval shaped, compact, with close-knit, well-arched toes. Pads are thick and resilient; nails short and strong. Rear dewclaws are removed.

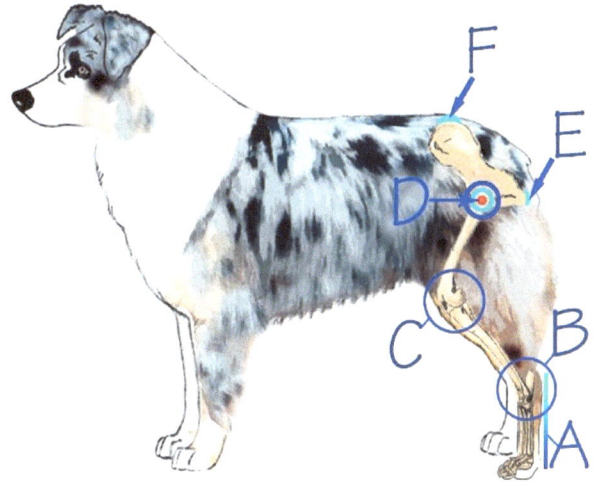

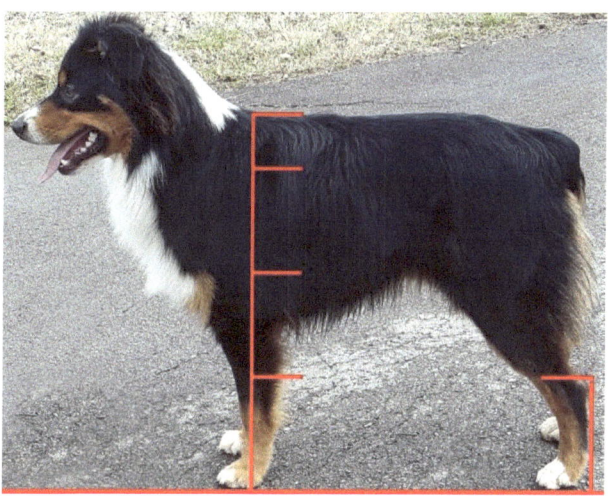

A – Rear pastern (metatarsi) commonly referred to as the hock.
B – Hock (tarsal) joint
C – Stifle joint
D – Hip joint and the center of gravity
E – Point of buttock (ishium)
F – Point of hip (iliac crest)

The length of the metatarsi (the hocks) determined by a ratio of 1:3 to 1:3.3 of shoulder height.

When the hock (tarsal) joint is correctly angled it places the rear foot under the vertical center of gravity of the rear assembly for optimal support. The hock and stifle are pictured in action below.

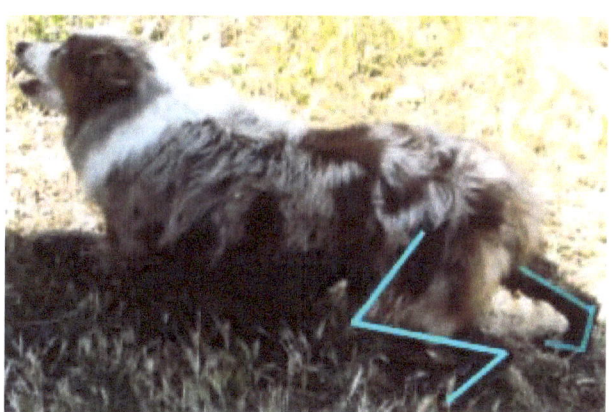

To correctly identify the dog's rear angulation, it's necessary for the hocks to be **vertical** to the ground on the side view.

There is a common misconception that MORE angulation contributes to better movement and less angulation is faulty. Why? Because the length of stride and length of time of the footfall on the ground correspond with speed. "Great sprinters do not have well-let-down hocks." – Curtis Brown.

Longer hocks provide leverage needed to get in and away from hooves and horns. They are also required to produce the quick bursts of speed to get ahead of stock.

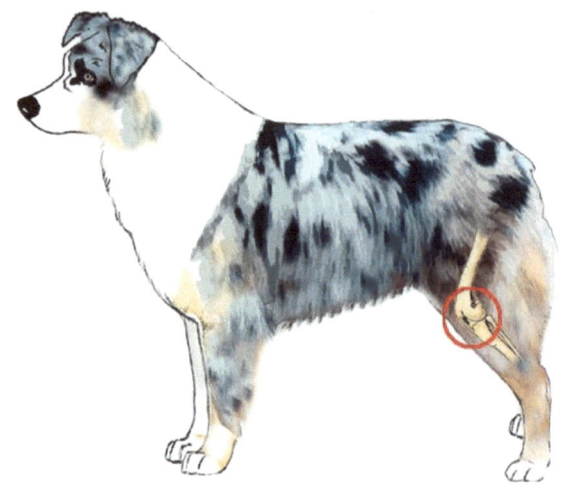

Notice the only point of contact (above) is the dog's hind foot. The rear assembly drives the dog into position transmitting power from the hindquarters through the loin to the forequarters.

The stifle or knee joint is the angle made between the upper thigh (femur) and the lower thigh (tibia and fibula). As the dog moves, the patella (like our knee cap) slides over the stifle joint.

The rear is the engine. It provides power and enables quick turns and ability to rollback and run in the opposite direction. The moderately bent stifle allows for sufficient length of both upper and lower thighs for good leg action. Longer metatarsi and well-developed rearing muscles of the loin and back legs are necessary for jumping high into the air to catch an airborne Frisbee disc or turn a heifer.

Moderate angulation is the most practical for Aussies for two reasons. There's a huge risk for injury with more angulation. Hindquarters with greater angulation are less stable because they lack vertical support. The rear assembly requires much more muscular strength especially when twisting and turning in deep sand, heavy snow, thick mud and on uneven terrain.

An Aussie using an easy canter to move a small herd of cattle. The breed must be able to go from a walk to a flat out run instantly.

The width of hindquarters is equal to the width of the forequarters at the shoulders. It's most evident from above.

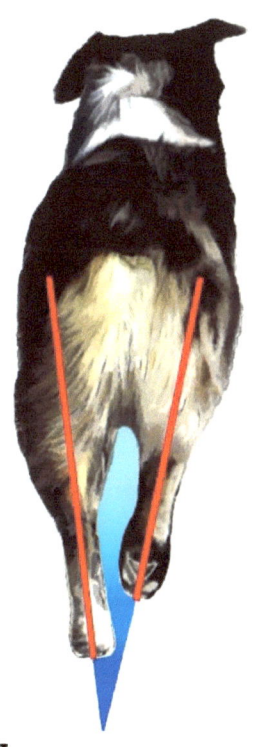

Going Away

As the dog is trotting away from the viewer, the feet converge toward the line of gravity (mid point) under the body. Simply put, the legs from the hip to paw resemble a "V" shape as the dog's legs are drawn underneath.

71

| Test Your Judging I.Q. |
| Hindquarters |

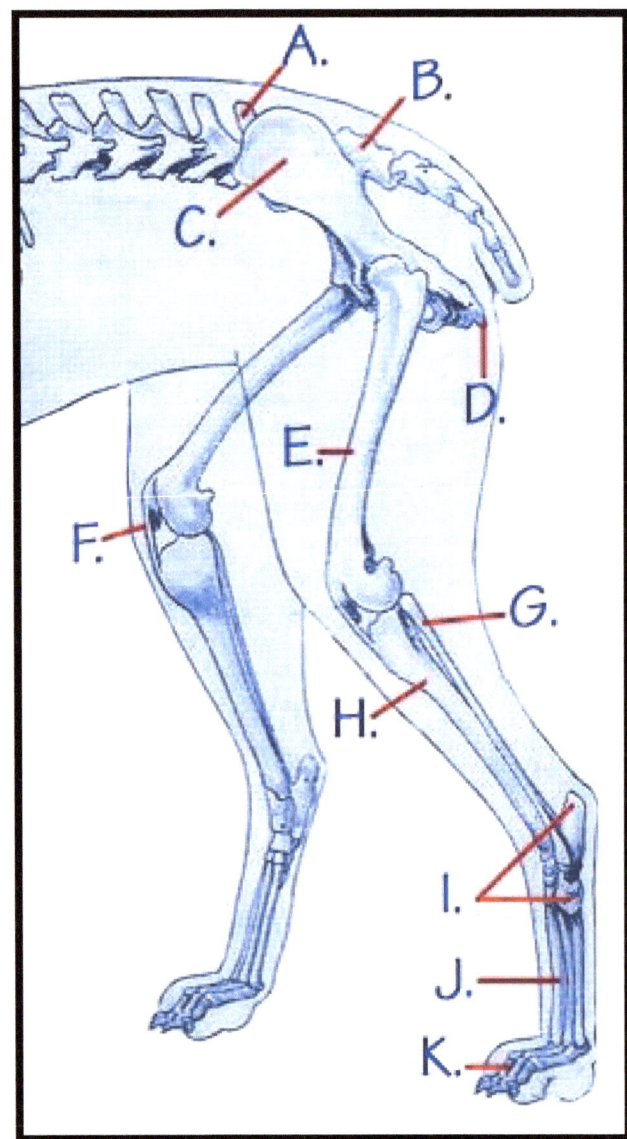

1. Match the above parts:

Sacrum	
Ischium	
Ilium	
Patella	
Fibula	
Tibia	
Hock (tarsal) joint	
Metatarsus	
Digits	
Femur	
Last Lumbar Vertebrae	

2. Can you list the hind limb counterparts to the front limb bones?

2a. Shoulder Blade
- 2a.

2b. Upper Arm (Humerus)
- 2b.

2c. Forearm (Radius and Ulna)
- 2c.

2d. Front Pastern (Metacarpals)
- 2d.

Word Bank

Bowed hocks, Close-behind, Correct hocks, Cow hocks.

Use the **Word Bank** above to write the term for hocks in motion:

3. Hocks that rotate inward towards the line of gravity:

_____

4. Hocks that rotate outward (away from) the line of gravity:

_____

5. Hocks with parallel placement along the line of gravity:

_____

6. Hocks that form a "V" from the line of gravity:

_____

Label the following illustrations using the answers above:

8. _____

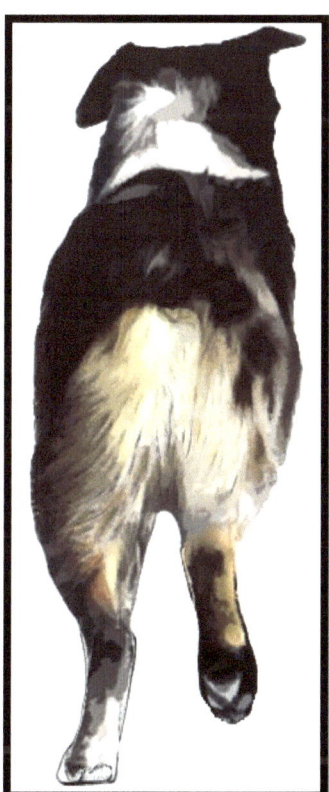

7. _____

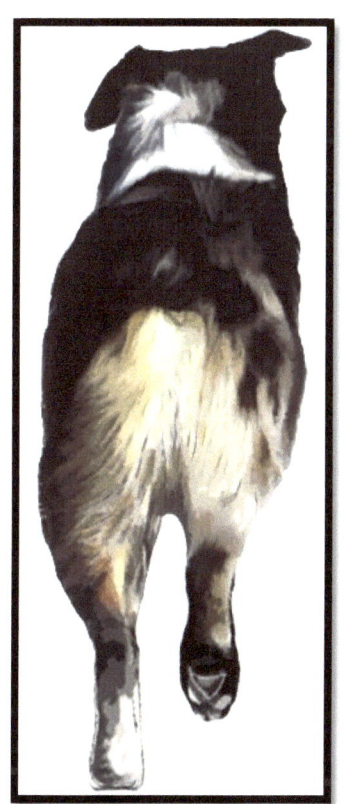

9. _____

10. The Aussie (**a**. or **b**.) is more able to gather itself to turn around and change gaits suddenly:

  a. When the plumb line drops from point of buttocks to the ground and the toes are under the pelvis.

OR

  b. When the plumb line drops down from the point of buttocks to the ground and the lower leg (metatarsus and foot) is under the pelvis?

11. ☐ True ☐ False. The pelvis is attached by a process of muscle and ligaments which allows for lateral mobility and shock absorption.

12. The hindquarters are designed for

  a. Weight bearing
  b. Driving

13. ☐ True ☐ False. The arrangement of the hock is similar to the pastern of the front leg.

14. In order for Aussies to turn swiftly and run in the opposite direction they must use their:

  a. Forequarters.
  b. Hindquarters.
  c. Both the above.

15. The most rearward section of the pelvis (ischium) is known as the

  a. Tail.
  b. Point of buttock or rump.
  c. Croup.
  d. Sacrum.

16. ☐ True ☐ False. The slope of the croup counterparts the slope of the pelvic girdle; therefore, the slope of the croup correctly indicates the set of the pelvis since it is anchored to it and is governed by its inner arch.

17. A steep pelvis usually aids:

  a. Rearward extension of the rear paw.
  b. Quickness and agility.

18. A flat pelvis usually aids:

  a. Rearward extension of the rear paw.
  b. Quickness and agility.

19. Over-angulation can occur from:

  a. A long tibia.
  b. A long femur.
  c. Too much bend in stifle.
  d. Flat croup.
  e. All of the above.
  f. None of the above.

20. The dog pictured in the above illustration is best suited:

    a. To sprint and pivot swiftly.
    b. For sustained trotting.

21. The dog pictured in the above illustration would be best suited for its ability:

    a. To sprint and pivot swiftly.
    b. For sustained trotting.

22. How can you determine the rear angulation of a dog?

    a. When the stifles are moderately bent.
    b. When the front legs and the hind legs parallel to each other.
    c. When the metatarsi are perpendicular to the ground.

23. What is the functional trade-off for an Australian Shepherd with well-let down (short, close to the ground) hocks (tarsal) joints, flatter pelvis and well laid-back shoulders versus an Aussie with longer hocks, a slightly steeper croup and pelvis?

    a. Sustained trotting efficiency.
    b. Quickness and agility.
    c. Turning ability.

24. ☐ True ☐ False. Long hocks (metatarsi) contribute to speed and agility.

25. ☐ True ☐ False. The hock height of the Australian Shepherd is a ratio of approximately 1:4 to 1:5 of shoulder height.

26. ☐ True ☐ False. The slope of the croup indicates the backward extension of the hind feet.

27. ☐ True ☐ False. Rear pasterns, the metatarsus is the same as the hocks.

28. When referring to hocks, what does well-let down mean?

    a. Metatarsi that are close to the ground.
    b. Metatarsi that are more distant from the ground.

29. ☐ True ☐ False. The croup angle is formed by the pelvic bone and the angle it forms when a straight line is drawn along the spine.

30. ☐ True ☐ False. The flatter angulation of the pelvis aids the Australian Shepherd in turn around efficiency.

31. Aussies with poorly developed rearing muscles are not as able to:

    a. Jump to catch a frisbee disc.
    b. Sprint to head off errant livestock.
    c. Trot.
    d. All the above.

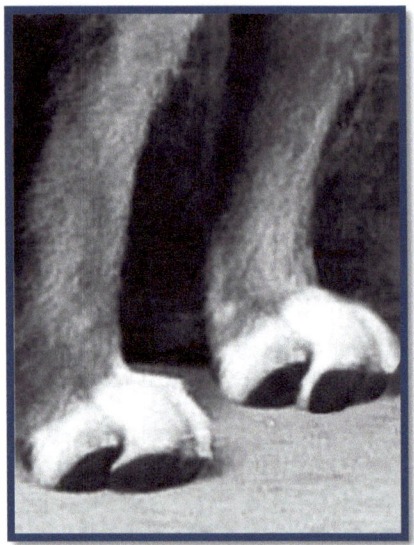

32. What causes a dog to rock back and stand on the heels of its feet (pictured above) instead of up on the pads?

    a. Straight stifles.
    b. Steep croup.
    c. The heart-shaped metatarsal pad is thin and poorly developed.
    d. The metatarsal pads are not under the line of gravity.

33. ☐ True ☐ False. Rear dewclaws attach to the other bones in the rear legs.

34. What is a skip step in the rear?

    a. Unique characteristic of the breed.
    b. Patellar luxation.
    c. When dog transitions from one speed to another.
    d. All the above.
    e. None of the above.

35. ☐ True ☐ False. In order for the stifles to be clearly defined they must be moderately bent.

36. ☐ True ☐ False. Hocks should be parallel to each other when viewed from the rear.

37. ☐ True ☐ False. The length of croup is associated with the length of hip.

38. ☐ Top or ☐ Bottom. Which Aussie is in a better position to go from a standstill to a sprint?

> ## Hindquarters Answers

1:
A. Last Lumbar Vertebrae.
B. Sacrum.
C. Ilium.
D. Ischium (point of buttock).
E. Femur.
F. Patella.
G. Fibula.
H. Tibia.
I. Hock (tarsal) joint.
J. Metatarsus.
K. Digits.

2:
2a-Pelvis.
2b- Upper Thigh (Femur).
2c-Lower Thigh (Tibia and Fibula).
2d- Metatarsus (Rear Pastern / Hock).

3-Cow hocks.
4-Bowed hocks.
5-Close-behind.
6-Correct.

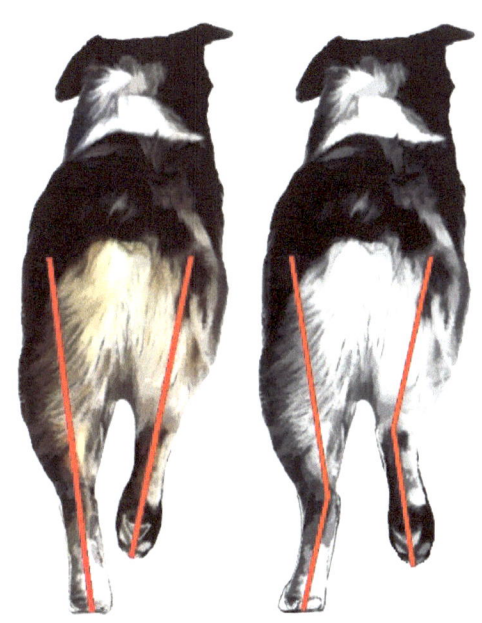

Correct hocks (left), 7-Cow hocked (right).

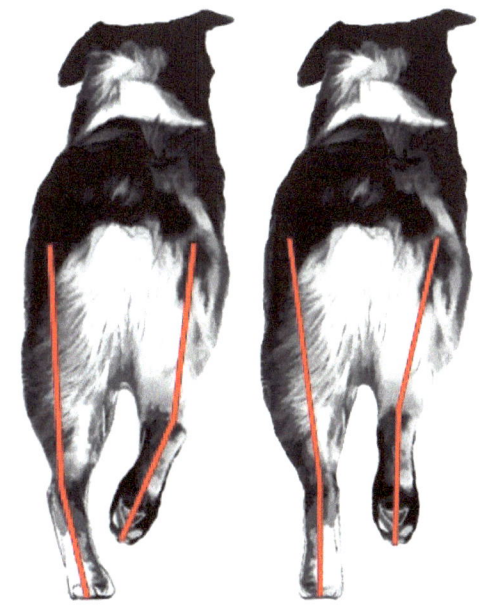

8-Bowed hocks (left), 9-Close-behind (right).

10-b. The Aussie with the (metatarsus and foot) under the pelvis has more accuracy for foot placement in turns and is able to turn more sharply than one with more angulation. The Supplement of Annotations to the original, 1977 Australian Shepherd Breed Standard stated, "The moderately bent (well-defined) stifle allows for sufficient length of both upper and lower thighs for good leg action and stride, while allowing a moderate bend to the hock joint for the metatarsi to drop straight with the pad of the foot directly under the vertical center of gravity of the rear assembly."

11-False. The pelvic limbs are attached directly to the vertebral column by ball-and-socket joints. The hip joint is formed where the thigh bone (femur) meets the bones that make up the pelvis. The pelvis is attached to the spinal column by sacrum.

12-b. The hindquarters (rear assembly) are designed for propulsion. They are the driving power that thrusts the Aussie into action.

13- True. The arrangement of the hock, also referred to as the rear pastern is comparable to the pastern of the front leg.

14-b. Dogs are dependent on the fore- and hindquarters working together. However, the hindquarters are mainly responsible for the dog's ability to stop abruptly, turn swiftly and run in the opposite direction.

15-b. Point of rump.

16-True.

17-b. Quickness and agility.

18-a. A flat pelvis usually aids rearward extension of the rear paw.

19-a and/or b or c. Aussies need enough flexibility for jumping and speed, but not so much bend (angulation) that quick turning ability is jeopardized.

20-b. For sustained trotting.

21-a. To sprint and pivot swiftly.

22-c. When the metatarsus (bones between hock and foot) is perpendicular to the ground.

23-b. The trade-off is quickness and agility. Clearly, the short, well-let-down metatarsi (hocks) called for in the breed standard contribute to the sustained, trotting efficiency.

24-True. Short hocks assist sustained trotting ability.

25-False. The ratio of the height of the hocks (rear pasterns) necessary for the Australian Shepherd to carry out its intended function is approximately 1:3.3 of shoulder height. Shorter hocks are not designed for the ability to change direction, swerve and feint or alter gait instantly.

26-True. A flatter pelvis is designed for sustained, long distance trotting, while steeper pelvic angles are designed for speed and agility.

27-False. The hock is actually the joint (tarsus) above the rear pastern. However, the rear pasterns are commonly referred to as the hocks as is practiced in this book.

28-a. Well let-down refers to short hocks (metatarsi) that are close to the ground.

29-True.

30-False. The slightly steeper angulation of the pelvis aids the breed in turn around efficiency.

31-a and b. Aussies with poorly developed rearing muscles of the loin and back legs are not as able to leap well or sprint to head off errant stock.

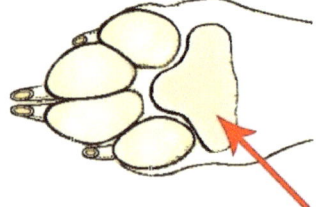

32-c. and d. The dog should always stand up on its toe (digital) and heel (metatarsal) pads. When the heel or plantar pads (central heart-shaped pads) are thin and poorly developed and/or the ligaments are lax, it causes the four smaller digital pads to tip upwards and shifts the dog's weight on the sesamoid bones rather than up on the pads. Consequently, the third digital bone isn't adequately supported and the dog's weight isn't uniformly dispersed. It also exposes the webbing to injury. **This should be faulted severely** since working dogs need sound feet to perform.

33-False. Rear dewclaws do **not** attach to other bones in the rear legs. Although five metatarsal bones contribute to the hocks, one known as the rear dewclaw is either absent or removed at birth.

34-b or c. A skip step – an intermittent hop - in the rhythm of the trot can be when the dog transitions from a walk (four beat gait) to a trot (two beat gait). A hitch in the gait can also be due to a patellar luxation. Patellar luxation can be congenital or trauma induced.

35-True. Additionally, hock action synchronizes with the stifle's action.

36-True. The hocks should be parallel and perpendicular to each other when viewed from the rear.

37-True. A fairly long croup is generally associated with a good length of the hip.

38-The top one. Both dogs are alert, poised and ready. The difference between them is the one on the top is positioned to go from a standstill to a sprint without hesitation. Why? Because its base of support is already under the center of gravity. The dog on the bottom must first draw its legs under itself before it can sprint.

Notes

Notes

 ## Gait

 ## Gait

The Australian Shepherd has a smooth, free and easy gait. He exhibits great agility of movement with a well balanced, ground covering stride. Fore and hind legs move straight and parallel with the center line of the body. As speed increases, the feet (front and rear) converge toward the center line of gravity of the dog while the back remains firm and level. The Australian Shepherd must be agile and able to change direction or alter gait instantly.

Smooth, free, and easy, exhibiting agility of movement with a well-balanced natural stride. As speed increases, both front and rear feet converge equally toward the centerline of gravity beneath the body. The topline remains firm and level. When viewed from the side the trot is effortless, exhibiting facility of movement rather than a hard driving action. Exaggerated reach and drive at the trot are not desirable. Gait faults shall be penalized according to the degree of deviation from the ideal.

1,500 reasons why movement counts.

In the real-world Aussies have to negotiate uneven, and sometimes rocky, terrain; very different than trotting across the level surface of a conformation ring. Balance and soundness is key in order for the dogs to do their job with less fatigue and avoid injuries.

Reach and drive. The hindquarters propel forward (above) while forequarters reach and stabilize (below).

Judges need to understand what is required of the breed in the real world. The biggest misunderstanding about the breed is Australian Shepherds are sustained trotting specialists. **They are not**. When livestock is moved in large numbers over long distances across varied terrain, Australian Shepherds are required to use all gaits from a walk, a slow jog, ordinary trot to a flat out run. Once the animals are under control and settled, the dogs will take the pressure off allowing the stock to move at a relaxed pace.

The above picture was taken during a fall roundup. There's an Australian Shepherd and three Livestock Guardian dogs (LGD). The LGD don't herd the sheep. They are part of the flock ready to defend their charges from predators. The stockdog on the other hand manages the entire flock. When everything is under control Aussies alternate from a walk to an average jog (pictured below) and then may sprint to turn back any sheep that stray off the trail. This is typical of Aussies doing this kind of work.

If one of the flock challenges the dog, then he or she must get out of harm's way and put the errant animal in its place.

The dog uses every aspect of its body from the head to the tail to avoid being hit as the ewe tries to butt him or her.

An Australian Shepherd with a sound, balanced trot should translate into an Aussie that can outmaneuver livestock. The trotting style is not choppy or stilted, but not long and flowing either. The trotting style is moderate. It has to be.

The angulation of femur attachment to the pelvis must coordinate with a non-specific shoulder and upper arm angulations for correct foot timing. They must be in harmony to produce a tireless gait.

Correct structure also means the dog can sprint and turn back runaways that have bolted from the herd. Aussies need the ability to stop, turn and make abrupt changes in directions.

Turning off the centerline. The dog's momentum is going one direction as indicated above by the black arrow. In order to turn 90 or 180 degrees midstride, the dog must pivot off the centerline (blue) and in the next stride sprint in the direction it just came from (red).

An example of an Aussie pivoting off the center line of the body to turn cows.

Changing directions in the middle of a stride (illustrated above).

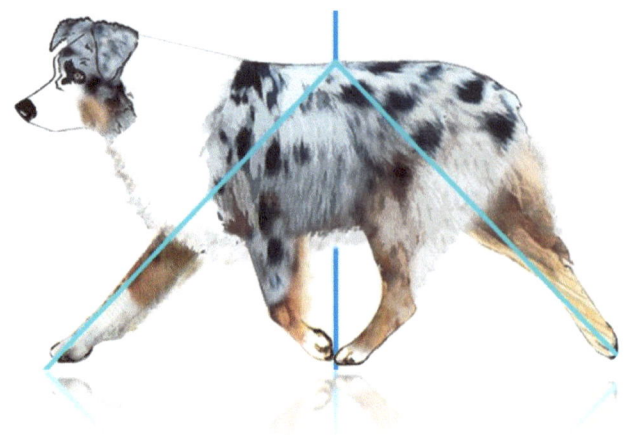

On page 117 of *Dog Locomotion and Gait Analysis,* Curtis Brown states: "Dog show enthusiasts, who are oriented toward showmanship, are apt to observe exaggerated, attractive trotting styles and then mistakenly apply that exaggerated style to many breeds. Several breeds have had their functional trotting style altered into a style designed to please the fancy, but not a style adapted to the breed's original function."

The forward and rearward extension are balanced one to the other. In other words, the forward reach equals the back stroke (backward reach). The hind leg follows through on the back stroke giving the rear legs adequate backward thrust.

Correct foot timing. The dog has normal strides of equal lengths. Both front feet and hind feet are synced to the weight-bearing foot. The front weight bearing foot leaves the ground a split-second before the hind foot "fills" its imprint. In other words, the hind foot should step into the print left by the front foot.

Good movement also means the dog moves from its shoulders and hips. Choppy gait is caused by an imbalance. The front and back angulation are not in harmony with each other. The front leg should not only reach forward but reach back without restriction.

As the front weight-bearing front foot leaves the ground, the hind foot moves into position to "fill" its place (as pictured above). Note: The next photo frame would catch the leading front foot as it contacts the ground. As a result the corresponding hind foot would reach its full extension in the backward stroke. Note the head carriage while working.

Over-driving causing the hind to reach beyond (over-reach) the front footprint.

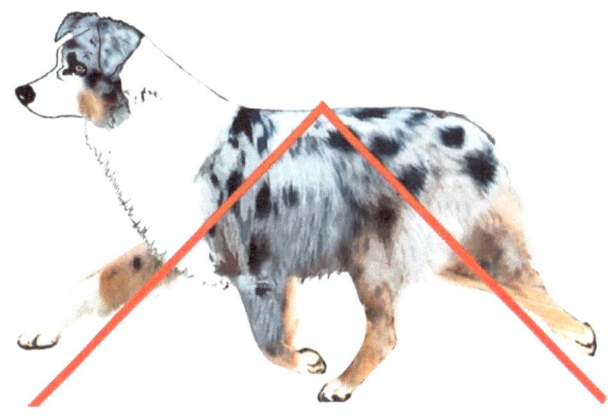

High action is wasted and inefficient for a stockdog. Wasted energy can lead to fatigue and injuries.

Balanced gait translates to athletic ability. Aussies swivel (pivot) from the center line, rather than pulling themselves around.

The only time it's acceptable for the hind paw to step beyond the foreprint is when the dog is turning to change directions such as moving laterally behind livestock (above). In this instance it's not over-driving.

When the hind feet consistently over-reach the front, problems such as crabbing, twisting the spine, and padding (also known as dwelling) are results due to more angulation and drive from behind than front.

Test Your Judging I.Q. Gait

1. What does the trotting gait reveal?

   a. Gait can be used to determine causes and location of lameness.
   b. Interplay between the fore and hind assemblies.
   c. Topline.
   d. Foot timing / foot fall.
   e. All the above.

2. ☐ True ☐ False. Length of stride is measured from the place where one paw leaves the ground to the place where the same paw again strikes the ground.

3. When trotting, the dog's front feet should reach to:

   a. Well in front of its chest.
   b. Beneath its nose.
   c. Well in front of its chest, but not beyond its nose.

4. When the rear hock (tarsal) joint hyperextends forward it's known as:

   a. Cow hocks.
   b. Sickle hocks.
   c. Slipped hocks.
   d. Double jointed.
   e. All the above.

5. Why should Australian Shepherds be exhibited on a loose lead?

   a. A tight lead puts pressure on the neck causing the dog to lift their front feet too high.
   b. A tight lead can cause the appearance of gaiting when none exist.
   c. A tight lead can disguise certain faults
   d. All the above.

6. ☐ True ☐ False. The Australian Shepherd is a long-distance trotting breed able to cover as much ground as possible with as few strides as necessary.

7. Australian Shepherds with the type of drivetrain for sustained trotting produce:

   a. Fewer strides per 100 feet than Australian Shepherds with the sprinting drivetrain at the same gait.
   b. More strides per 100 feet than Aussies with the sprinting drivetrain at the same gait.

8. Australian Shepherds with a sprinting drivetrain:

   a. Lack efficient trotting ability.
   b. Have a different trotting style.
   c. Are more capable to sprint than trot.
   d. All the above.

9. Rolling gait refers to:

   a. The easy-going gait of a long-distance trotter.
   b. Swaying ambling action of the hindquarters in motion.
   c. Lumbering gait.

10. ☐ Hackney gait or ☐ Padding. When the front feet flip upward on the forward reach.

11. ☐ Hackney gait or ☐ Padding? When the dog's front feet are lifted upwards while flexing the pastern and toe points downwards.

12. What causes padding?

   a. Over angulation in the rear assembly.
   b. Over angulation in the forequarters.

13. ☐ True ☐ False. The Aussie's front and rear legs are parallel to each other (straight columns of vertical support) when standing. At a trot they converge toward the line of gravity as speed increases.

14. ☐ True ☐ False. Crabbing can lead to orthopedic problems.

15. Identify the above gait:

   a. Flying trot.
   b. Over-driving.
   c. Pacing.
   d. Hackney-like.

16. What is over-drive?

   a. A synonym used for the flying trot.
   b. Crabbing.
   c. The dog has excessive angulation in the forequarters.
   d. The dog's hind feet over-reach (step beyond) the front feet.

17. Over-reach is caused by or when:

   a. Long legs.
   b. Short body.
   c. Height at withers exceeds body length.
   d. Being gaited faster than a practical speed.
   e. More angulation and drive from behind than front.
   f. All the above.

18. ☐ True ☐ False. Over-reach is acceptable as long as the dog doesn't crab.

19. When a dog over drives what problem(s) are caused?

   a. Twisting the spine.
   b. Crabbing or padding
   c. Both the above.

20. Which of the following statements is true?

   a. The dog's angulation determines foot placement.
   b. The dog's body length determines foot placement.
   c. The dog's body length determines foot placement, which is governed by angulation.

21. Which trait is the most important for the tireless trot?

   a. Good foot timing.
   b. Long reach and drive.
   c. Longer body length to height ratio.

22. When the hind foot is unable to "fill" the front track:

   a. Long body.
   b. Short legs.
   c. Angulation in the hindquarter isn't balanced to the forequarters.
   d. Any or all the above.

23. ☐ True ☐ False. The dog in the above illustration is in balance with itself exhibiting good reach and drive.

24. Correct transition between the front and rear quarters is indicated by:

   a. Visible action at the withers.
   b. Minimal action at the withers.

25. ☐ True ☐ False. A peculiar flip in the front feet is a unique trait of the breed.

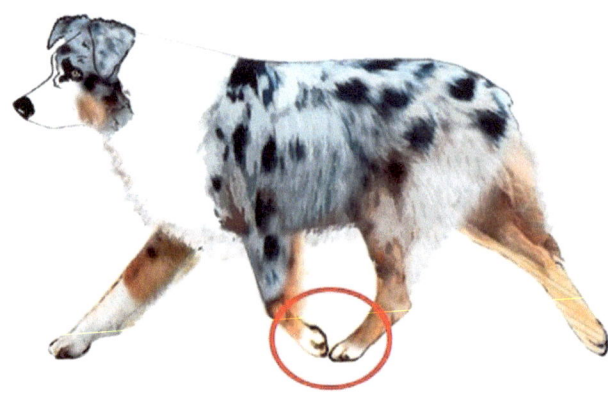

26. ☐ True ☐ False. The dog in the above illustration has correct foot timing.

27. If we judge with the theory Australian Shepherds are a true working breed, a judge should:

   a. Disregard dirty, unkept coats.
   b. Fault dogs that aren't fit and in working condition.

28. What causes a dog to roll across the topline as it trots?

   a. Immaturity.
   b. Unique breed trait.
   c. Joint laxity.
   d. Loose connective tissue.
   e. Poor physical fitness.

29. The slightly steeper angles (when viewed from the side) of working and performance Australian Shepherds are due to:

   a. Poor conformation.
   b. Unsoundness.
   c. Lacking quality.
   d. None of the above.

30. Handlers use a tight lead to:

   a. Shift the weight off the front assembly.
   b. Hide a fault.
   c. Create expression in a dog that cannot lift its own ears.
   d. All the above.
   e. None of the above.

31. There's a current trend for long-bodied Australian Shepherds to be exhibited in the show ring. Why?

   a. Judges misinterpret the "slightly longer than tall" part of the standard.
   b. The rear foot can have greater reach without interfering with the front feet.

32. ☐ True ☐ False. It's not unusual for an Australian Shepherd to drop its head (and neck) level with their topline while working stock at a trot.

Gait Answers

1-e. All the above.

2-True.

3-c. The dog's front foot should reach in front of its chest, but not beyond its nose. If an Aussie's front feet reach beyond the nose at the trot indicates over angulation.

4-c and/or d. Hock (tarsal) joint normally flex and bend. The hocks have a good range of motion, but when the joint hyperextends (bends forward) it's because there's laxity in the ligaments that stabilize the hock joint. The joint can be easily pushed forward when standing. It wobbles and creates instability and is highly detrimental to the working dog. There may even be a cruciate problem at the knee. Continued on page 89:

Sickle hocks (metatarsal pad is placed below the hip joint) are not a serious fault unless the ligaments of hocks don't allow full extension in the back swing thus limiting rear leg extension.

5-d. All the above.

6-False: The historical function of the breed is to work livestock. In order for the Aussie to perform the tasks of his original function he must be able to trot for certain distances as well as make instantaneous gait changes, quick and sudden turns and abrupt stops over varied terrain in close proximity to hooves and horns.

7-a. Australian Shepherds with the type of drivetrain built for sustained trotting produce fewer strides per 100 feet than Aussies built for sprinting.

8-b. Australian Shepherds with a sprinting drivetrain do not lack efficient trotting ability. They have a **different trotting style** than Aussies built for sustained trotting. Efficient trotting ability is dependent on soundness and balance.

9-b or c. Rolling or a lumbering gait is undesirable in Aussies because it's cloddy instead of quick and agile.

10- Padding. Padding occurs when the dog's front feet swing upward in a delaying action on the forward reach. The toe is pointed downwards in hackney gait when the wrist is flexed.

11-Hackney gait.

12-a. Padding also known as *dwelling* is caused when the front is overdriven from the rear. The front feet flex upward in a pause or delayed action to avoid impact from the rear. It helps synchronize the forelegs with longer stride from behind.

13-True. The front and rear legs are like straight colums of vertical support.

14-True. When a dog crabs it is moving off line (causing the spine to twist) to avoid leg interference from the hind feet with front feet.

15-c. Pacing. The pace is a lateral gait where the left front and left hind legs move in unison and then the right front and right hind legs move in unison. The center of gravity shifts from side to side.

16-d. Over-drive is when a dog's hind feet over-reach the front feet. Dogs that over-drive may crab, but not in every case. Crabbing is when the dog moves offline twisting the spinal column.

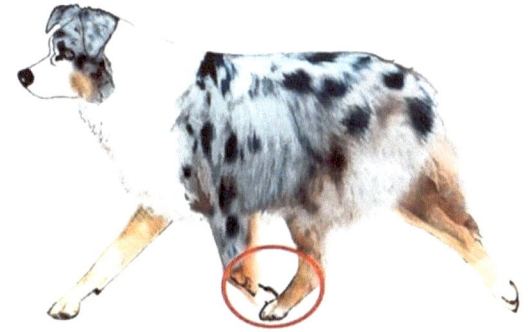

17-f. Over-reach (overdriving) can be caused by any of all the above. Instead of the hind foot "filling" the track of the fore print, it causes the front feet and legs to get out of the way of the back ones to "side-step" the fore print thus creating a new track.

18-False. Over-reach, though commonly seen in show dogs, can make it difficult for a dog to transition from one gait to another or pivot on the center line. Therefore, over-reach is a fault.

19-c. Problems such as crabbing, twisting the spine, and padding also known as dwelling. Overdriving causes the dog to compensate (delay the action) to keep the hind feet from interfering with the weight-bearing front foot.

20-c. Body length determines foot placement, which is governed by angulation.

21-a. The Australian Shepherd's ability to "trot all day long" is dependent on good foot timing regardless if it is an Aussie with a sprinting drivetrain or an Aussie with a trotting drivetrain.

22-d. Any or all the above. An Aussie that lacks the reciprocating angulation of the front assembly complementing the driving hindquarters cannot "fill" his fore tracks and ends up wasting energy. Some dogs take short steps to avoid crabbing or clipping (striking the front foot).

23- False. The Aussie in the above illustration is **not** in balance with itself. The dog is showing more reach in the front than in the rear.

24-b. Minimal up and down movement or bobbing as the withers should remain fairly level.

25-False. The flip is a fault known as paddling.

26-True. The dog in the illustration has correct foot timing.

27-b. Fault dogs that aren't in working condition. Unkept, dirty coats and/or teeth is offensive. It is in no way a representation of a dog's status as a working dog.

28-d. One of the main reasons mature Aussies roll across the topline is looseness of connective tissue (collagenous fibers within and around the muscles under the skin).

Connective tissue that forms the body's supportive framework provides structure and strength to the muscles and skin. Aussies that are soft and flabby lack muscle tone and definition. **This is a fault.** It's also an inherited trait and unable to be improved with exercise.

29-d. None of the above. The breed's tendency for slightly straighter shoulders (not straight), a little steeper croup, longer pelvis and longer hocks which produces a shorter-quicker stride is due to the breed's original, historic function as a quick and agile stockdog.

There is a popular misconception that slightly steeper angles indicate incorrect angles and therefore produce faulty gait. As long as the individual is in balance (angulation of the forequarters is in harmony with the hindquarters) the gait will be in balance.

30-b. A tight lead can cause unnatural gait such as the front legs to lift higher than they would normally. Some handlers use a tight lead to hide a fault. Inexperienced handlers can cause the appearance of a fault when none exists.

31-b. The longer body is helpful for dogs that mainly trot because the rear feet can have longer reach without hitting with the front feet. However, long bodies are **not** correct for the breed and should be faulted accordingly.

32-True. See the pictures on page 91. It's not a fault or unusual for an Aussie to carry its head level with its topline while working at a trot. Dogs that have low head and neck carriage due to weak muscling move laboriously. It's not light and agile, but heavy.

Aussies may drop their head and neck while working at a trot. As a point of reference: see the carriage of same dog's head and neck above and pictured below while jumping and in a natural stance looking for cows.

 ## Coat

 ## Coat

Hair is of medium texture, straight to wavy, weather resistant and of medium length. The undercoat varies in quantity with variations in climate. Hair is short and smooth on the head, ears, front of forelegs and below the hocks. Backs of forelegs and britches are moderately feathered. There is a moderate mane and frill, more pronounced in dogs than in bitches. Non-typical coats are *severe faults*.

The coat is of medium length and texture, straight to slightly wavy, and weather resistant. The undercoat varies in quantity with climate. Hair is short and smooth on the head, outside of ears, front of forelegs, and below the hocks. Backs of forelegs are moderately feathered and breeches are moderately full. There is a moderate mane, more pronounced in dogs than bitches. The Australian Shepherd is a working dog and is to be shown with a natural coat.

Severe Faults: Non-typical coats such as excessively long; overabundant /profuse; wiry; or curly.

The Aussie's coat is not simply an item of great beauty, but one of utility. It should not be forgotten that the coat is a protective covering against all elements. The coat texture and its quality are as important as its length and quantity. The ideal coat is one of low maintenance, due partly to its moderate length, but equally due to the dirt repelling texture. Dirt should brush out easily and mud should fall off when it dries. The Aussie's hair coat should make you think of wash and wear.

The coat is straight to slightly wavy. The length is easily observed by sight. Moderate means kept or keeping within proper limits, not extreme or excessive. Take a look at foundation dogs such as Champion Nifty Nubbins of Flintridge (pictured above) to understand what moderate actually meant to the drafters of the original 1977 Breed Standard.

The length of the hair covering is governed by genetic inheritance. The quality and density of the hair coat is influenced by environment. There is great diversity among the type of hair coats between breeds in the dog world, even among the herding group. While the coat can be a thing of beauty, it must be considered for its function. Hair is a protector, and a temperature regulator. The coat of the Australian Shepherd was developed in the ranch country by selecting the qualities that proved to meet the demands of the pastoral environment with a minimum of maintenance.

When considering environmental conditions in fields and pastures such as the presence of brush, drooping brome, cockleburs, sandburs, grass awns which can work through the coat and into the skin along with mud, rain and heat, you cannot have a coat that requires tedious grooming. This is not to say the Aussie's coat is maintenance free, because none are. Mud, burrs, snowballs collect more frequently in longer, woolly, dense, wiry, curly or extremely fine coats and is more difficult to remove. Smooth, slick coats are uncharacteristic of the breed.

The guard hair or outer coat provides protection against sunburn, and to a certain degree protects against insect bites. The downy undercoat insulates the Australian Shepherd against cold temperatures and will commensurate with climatic conditions. The Aussie's ability to shed or grow undercoat enhances his utility in a variety of climates. An Aussie working for long hours under a Texas sun will not develop the same undercoat as an Australian Shepherd during a Canadian winter. The length of the outer coat will not change however with the weather or amount of daylight.

Sculpting Coats

The trend of shaping coats is detrimental to the breed. Why? Because it's dishonest. Sculpting alters the coat and the overall appearance. It can be used to disguise excessively long, overabundant (profuse) coats and conceal or minimize structural faults. What you see is not what you get genetically. The show ring is supposed to help determine the genetic future of the breed.

Whiskers

The whiskers around the eyes and muzzle are extremely sensitive and have a rich nerve supply.

Whiskers are sensors that are necessary for the stockdog to gauge the precise distances from the face to the point of contact with stock when performing dangerous work such as gripping heels and dodging horns.

Excerpts from **The Total Australian Shepherd: Beyond the beginning** by Carol Ann Hartnagle and Ernest Hartnagle: "Whiskers, the stiff hairs (vibrissae) on the muzzle, should never be trimmed, because they serve a vital sensory function. The vibrissae are constructed anatomically much differently from other body hair. They are deeply rooted in erectile tissue that is served by sensory nerve fibers and act as levers on the nerves that serve them." According to Dr. Thomas E. McGill, "The vibrissae in dogs are more heavily innervated than other body hair, that is, more nerve fibers serve such vibrissa. The vibrissae in dogs are served by the trigeminal nerve, the largest of the twelve pairs of canine cranial nerves – larger than the optic nerve, auditory nerve, or olfactory nerve." – Page 143.

We've seen the behavioral effects firsthand. In the early 1970s it was not uncommon for all Aussies to work and show. Conformation shows were held the first day of an ASCA Specialty and Stock Dog trials were held on the second day. All Aussies could compete in both venues (and many did). We trimmed Las Rocosa Leslie CSD including her whiskers for the first day of competition. She won and earned the point necessary for her Championship.

The next day was the Stock Dog Trial. In the cattle class she refused to heel – even though she was a highly seasoned cowdog with tons of experience working cattle in the real world. We had never seen her refuse to head or heel anything except when her whiskers were removed. She instinctively knew that she was vulnerable to injury without her whiskers to help gauge the distance when going in to heel. That was the only time it ever happened. She was fine as soon as her whiskers grew out.

In all our years, judging, showing, working and trialing we've never heard of a real reason to remove sensory whiskers from the muzzle of any dog. It's a senseless and even cruel practice. Whiskers are necessary for the dog's physical and psychological well-being.

Conclusion: "The whiskers (vibrissae) are served by the trigeminal nerves contributing to important sensory functions used by stockdogs and should never be trimmed."

Test Your Judging I.Q.
Coat

1. What guideline did the drafters of the original 1977 ASCA breed standard use when they described the coat as medium length and moderate?

    a. The Complete Dog Book.
    b. The AKC Guide for Writing Breed Standards.
    c. The early foundation dogs.
    d. The Dog in Action.

2. What is moderate length coat mean?

    a. Midway between long and smooth.
    b. Sensible and restrained.
    c. Long in winter, short in summer.
    d. Easy grooming.
    e. Weather resistant.

3. ☐ AKC ☐ ASCA? Which breed standard states, "The Australian Shepherd is a working dog and is to be shown with a natural coat."

4. ☐ True ☐ False. Grooming practices that make the dog look like it has large bone should not be rewarded.

5. ASCA emphasizes the Australian Shepherd is a working dog and is to be shown with a natural coat. What does that mean?

    a. Brush and bathe the dog.
    b. Trimming to neaten up the outside of the ears, the feet, below the hocks and back of front pasterns or the flag on the tail.
    c. Mud or dirt in the coat is acceptable because it's a working dog.
    d. All the above.

6. ☐ True ☐ False. Excessive grooming using scissors or substances to alter the coat or overall appearance is deceptive.

Coat Answers

1-c. Go to the first chapter on history and look at what was meant by medium length and moderate. The context used was in reference to the foundation dogs themselves.

2-b. Sensible and restrained. Weather-resistant refers to the texture which should protect from elements and help repel dirt and debris from becoming embedded and entangled. Heavy coats can easily become matted and a safe haven for ticks and fleas.

3-ASCA.

4-True. Because it's untypical of the breed. Grooming practices that sculpt the hair are perpetuating an unnatural look.

5-a, and/or b. The Australian Shepherd is a working dog and is to be shown with a natural coat. That means, the Aussie should be clean and neat. Trimming is allowed to tidy up stray hair outside of the ears, the feet, below the hocks, behind the front pasterns or flag on the tail.

6-True. When the coat is highly trimmed one might assume the practice is being done to disguise a non-typical coat which is a severe fault and should not be ignored or rewarded.

The practice of trying to deceive the viewer's eye by creating the look of large bone, round feet, changing the angle of the croup or reshaping the bottom or underline should also not be ignored or rewarded.

For the record: A dirty coat and/or teeth should never be misconstrued as a feature of a working stockdog. It's not so. Along with an unsoiled, well brushed coat, an Aussie's teeth should be clean as well. It's a matter of health and good hygiene!

 ## Color

 ## Color

Blue merle, black, red merle, red – all with or without white markings and/or tan (copper) points, with no order of preference. The hairline of a white collar does not exceed the point of the withers at the skin. White is acceptable on the neck (either in part or as a full collar), chest, legs, muzzle, underparts, blaze on head and white extension from underpart up to four inches, measuring from a horizontal line at the elbow. White on the head should not predominate, and the eyes must be fully surrounded by color and pigment. Merles characteristically become darker with increasing age.

Disqualifications – White body splashes, which means white on body between withers and tail, on sides between elbows and back of hindquarters in all colors.

All colors are strong, clear and rich. The recognized colors are blue merle, red (liver) merle, solid black, and solid red (liver) all with or without white markings and/or tan (copper) points with no order of preference.

On all colors the areas surrounding the ears and eyes are dominated by color other than white. The hairline of a white collar does not exceed the point at the withers.

Disqualifications: Other than recognized colors. White body splashes. Dudley nose.

Nose – Blue merles and blacks have black pigmentation on the nose (and lips). Red merles and reds have liver (brown) pigmentation on the nose (and lips).

On the merles it is permissible to have small pink spots; however, they should not exceed 25% of the nose on dogs over one year of age, which is a ***serious fault***.

The blue merle and black have black pigmentation on nose, lips and eye-rims. Reds and red merles have liver pigmentation on nose, lips and eye rims.

Butterfly nose should not be faulted under one year of age.

Blacks and blue merles have black pigmentation on the nose, lips and eye-rims. Blue merles are actually black dogs with merle patterns. Their coats can vary from tiny freckles to large, bold patches.

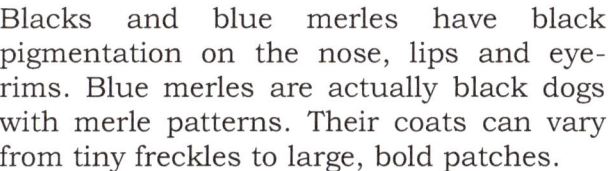

Reds and red merles can range from deep chestnut to "sorrel." The merle patterns vary from a roan base with tiny flecks, to large speckles. All have liver (brown) pigmentation on nose, lips and eye rims.

The blue merle pup (left) has a black nose, lips and eye rims. The deep red merle in the middle that's almost burgandy in hue and the pup on the right both have a liver nose and eye rims. The cinnamon and sugar color on the far right will mature into a silvery red merle with liver pigmentation.

An example of a deep, dark liver coated dog on the left (above).

The standards call for color to surround the eyes and ears. Pigment is important in the working Australian Shepherd. Aussies with deep, rich color are more likely to have normal eye and nose pigment. Aussies with light pigment and unpigmented skin are more prone to sunburn and skin cancer than those with dark pigment. The lack of pigmentation in certain important areas such as the **inner** ears and eye rims can be problematic because it can cause deafness and light sensitivity.

Pink eye rims are not listed as a disqualification but are faulted because it departs from the ideal and has potential health risks for Aussies working outdoors exposed to ultraviolet (UV) radiation.

An example of a rich, sorrel or chestnut red with liver pigmentation (above).

White Markings

Acceptable white trim in Australian Shepherds is usually the result of what is commonly acknowledged as the Irish Spotting gene. It can appear on the tail tip (in tailed Aussies), tip of the muzzle, tips of the paws and the breastbone. It can cover the muzzle, the topskull, front of the chest, and the lower legs. It can also extend from the front to the back of the neck and up the legs.

Aussies that also carry the piebald gene may have white that extends further up the hind legs onto the stifles, the dog's knee and under the belly.

Since the hair tips of a white collar can extend beyond the hairline at the withers, judges must part the coat and view the origin of the roots **on the skin**.

> **ASCA:** On all colors the areas surrounding the ears and eyes are dominated by color other than white. The hairline of a white collar does not exceed the point at the withers.

> **Disqualifications:** White body splashes.

On all colors (merle or solid), white collars are allowed on the neck and chest as defined by the vertical line. It's also allowed on the front legs, under the belly and on the hind legs the same as tan (copper) trim.

White body splashes are white areas (patches or spots, an island of white) on the body between the point of withers to the point of buttocks occurring on any color.

The reason behind the disqualification is due to the fact white markings can be the result of the double merle gene. Double merles have large amounts of white on their coats and faces predisposing the dog to deafness and certain eye anomalies.

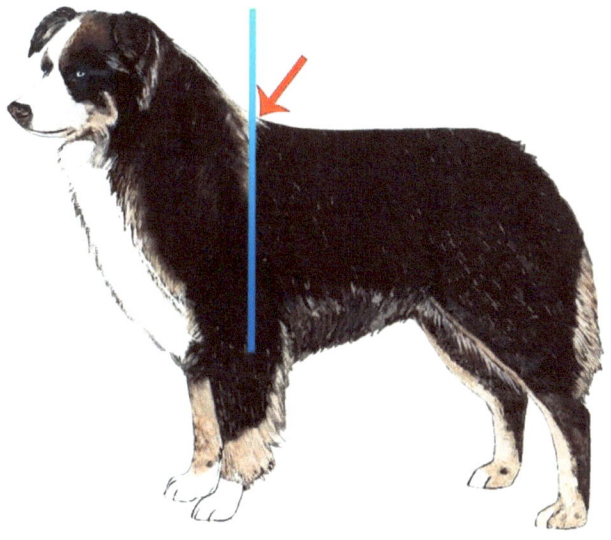

> **AKC:** White is acceptable on the neck (either in part or as a full collar), chest, legs, muzzle, underparts, blaze on head and white extension from underpart up to four inches, measuring from a horizontal line at the elbow.

Disqualifications – White body splashes, which means white on body between withers and tail, on sides between elbows and back of hindquarters in all colors.

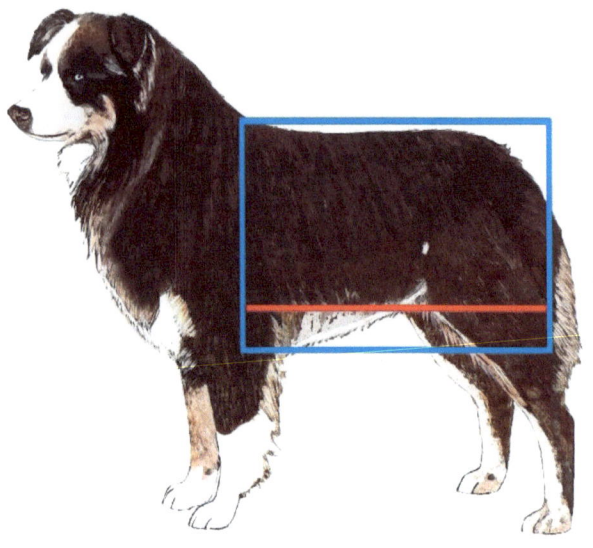

AKC educational material **contradicts** the standard's description of "white body splashes". They construe white that extends into the body (red rectangular area) is not the same as "white on the body between the withers and tail" which is listed as a **disqualification.** The material puts forward: White markings extending into the red area are to be considered **faults.**

Asymmetrical Markings

The beauty of the Australian Shepherd is the wide variation of colors and markings. Some Aussies have symmetrical collars and blazes and some have uneven markings. Neither breed standard prefers symmetrical nor penalizes asymmetrical markings. It's important for judges not to fault a dog where there is no fault listed in the breed standard.

Certain markings can create incorrect impressions such as more or less angulation. For example, the vertical merle pattern on the Aussie in above illustration may appear as though the dog has upright shoulders. Other markings can make it look like a dog has faults where none exist.

Test Your Judging I.Q.
Color

1. ☐ True ☐ False. White on the ear can cause deafness.

2. Acceptable colors are blue merle, solid black, red merle, or solid red with:

   a. Blue merle being most desirable.
   b. No order of preference.
   c. Blue and red merle being most desirable.
   d. White markings and/ or tan points being most desirable.

3. ☐ True ☐ False. Red merles may have black and/or liver pigmentation on their noses.

4. What would you do if you were judging the dog with a gray nose in the above picture?

   a. Fault the dog because it doesn't have black pigmentation on the nose and eye rims.
   b. Disqualify the dog because it is not an acceptable color.

5. What is a Dudley nose (a, b, c or d)?

   a. Pink spots.
   b. Butterfly nose.
   c. Unpigmented.
   d. Dilute.

6. ☐ True ☐ False. A dudley nose is a serious fault.

7. What is a Butterfly nose?

   a. Dark and light pigmentation.
   b. Unpigmented nose leather.
   c. Nose leather with areas lacking pigmentation.

8. ☐ True ☐ False. Butterfly nose is a disqualification in ASCA.

9. ☐ True ☐ False. The butterfly nose is considered a serious fault in AKC on dogs over one year of age only if it exceeds 25%.

10. In AKC, it is acceptable for Australian Shepherds to have small pink spots on the nose leather, however they should not exceed:

   a. 50% of the nose leather.
   b. 25% of the nose leather.
   c. 75% of the nose leather.

11. An individual exceeding the acceptable limit of unpigmented nose leather would be considered:

   a. A serious fault.
   b. A disqualification.
   c. No preference is made.

12. The nose on the left (above) is fully pigmented. The nose on the right is called:

   a. Butterfly nose exceeding 25%.
   b. Dudley nose.

13. ☐ AKC ☐ ASCA. Dudley nose is listed as a disqualification.

14. ☐ AKC ☐ ASCA. "Butterfly nose should not be faulted under one year of age."

15. ☐ AKC ☐ ASCA. "On the merles it is permissible to have small pink spots; however, they should not exceed 25% of the nose on dogs over one year of age, which is a *serious fault*."

16. Acceptable white trim that occurs in the Australian Shepherd due to:

    a. Irish spotting.
    b. Homozygous merle.
    c. Merle gene.
    d. Heterochromia.

17. ☐ True ☐ False. A blue merle is actually a black dog with a merle pattern.

18. ☐ True ☐ False. The hairline of the white collar is determined by looking at the skin where the hairline originates.

19. ☐ True ☐ False. Stifle white is disqualified in ASCA.

20. ☐ True ☐ False. The ASCA standard disqualifies dogs with white coming up from under the belly.

21. ☐ True ☐ False. White that extends beyond four inches above the elbow is <u>not</u> faulted in AKC.

22. ☐ True ☐ False. The eyes may be surrounded by color (black or liver pigmentation).

23. ☐ True ☐ False. A cryptic merle is able to be identified by the merle pattern in its coat or on its tail.

24. Australian Shepherds may have:

    a. Tan points.
    b. White trim.
    c. Tan and/or white markings.
    d. No trim.
    e. Tan and/or white or no trim at all.

25. ☐ True ☐ False. Aussies come in two different patterns. How many different color combinations may be exhibited in Aussies?

    a. 24.
    b. 16.
    c. 8.
    d. 12.
    e. 20.

Color Answers

1-False. Extreme white can cause deafness when there is a lack of pigment in parts of the inner ear. Judges are unable to determine this because it's not visible in the show ring.

2-b. No order of preference.

3-False. Red merles have liver pigmentation on their noses.

4-b. Disqualify the dog. The ASCA standard states dogs should be disqualified if they are an unacceptable color. Both breed standards state the Australian Shepherd must have black pigmentation on the nose leather and eye rims.

5-c. Unpigmented.

6-False. A Dudley nose is a disqualification in ASCA.

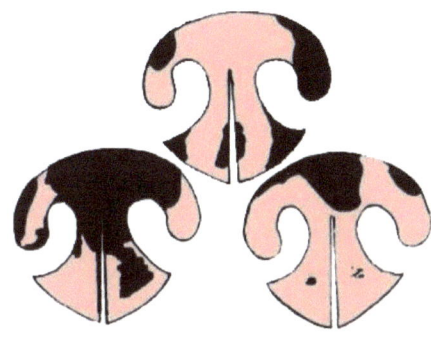

7-c. A Butterfly nose is nose leather with areas lacking pigmentation.

8-False. The butterfly nose in ASCA is not to be faulted under one year of age.

9-True. If there is 25% of non-pigmented (pink) skin on dogs over a year of age.

10-b. They should not exceed 25% of the nose leather.

11-a. A serious fault.

12-Dudley. Nose leather without pigmentation.

13-ASCA.

14-ASCA.

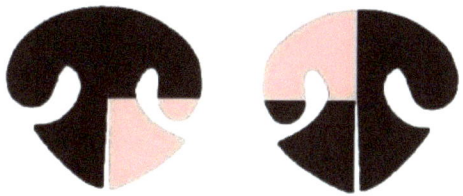

15-AKC. Pink spots should not exceed 25% (¼) of the nose on dogs over one year of age, which is a serious fault.

16-a. Irish spotting.

17-True. A blue merle is a black dog with a merle pattern. The same is true for a red merle. Red merles are liver colored dogs with merle patterns.

18-True. The hairline is determined at the roots where the hairline originates.

19-False. White can appear on the stifles in the same way tan (copper) trim can.

20-False. White is allowed under the belly and on the hind legs the same as tan (copper) trim.

21-False. White that extends beyond four inches above the elbow is severely faulted.

22-False. The eyes <u>must be</u> (not may be) fully surrounded by color.

23-False. A cryptic merle is a genetic merle that may appear as a solid red or black dog. Merles often get darker with age, so if merle coloring is visible in the coat it can become barely recognizable or obscured. Sometimes the only indication of merle is on a tail that may have been docked at birth.

24-e. Tan and/or white, or no trim at all.

25-True. c.-16. Aussies are either solid or merle with 16 different color combinations.

 ## Size

Size – The preferred height for males is 20-23 inches, females 18-21 inches. Quality is not to be sacrificed in favor of size. *Proportion* – Measuring from the breastbone to rear of thigh and from top of the withers to the ground the Australian Shepherd is slightly longer than tall. *Substance* – Solidly built with moderate bone. Structure in the male reflects masculinity without coarseness. Bitches appear feminine without being slight of bone.

 ## Size

Preferred height at the withers for males is 20 to 23 inches; that for females is 18 to 21 inches, however, quality is not to be sacrificed in favor of size.

Other Disqualifications: Monorchidism and cryptorchidism

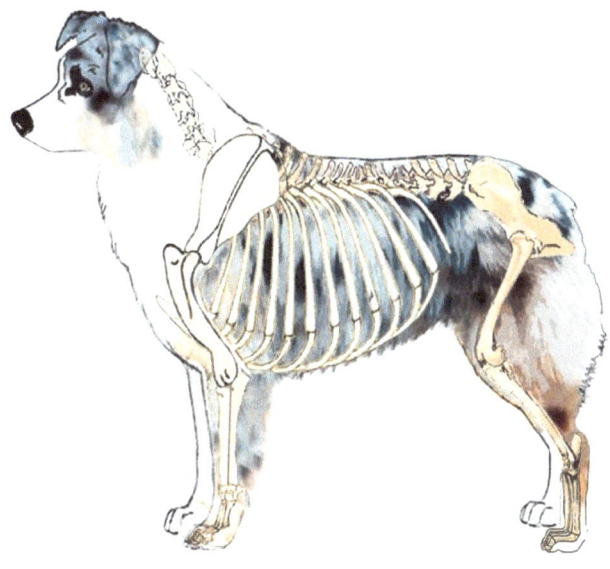

Moderate: The section on size repeats certain traits described earlier under **General Appearance**. Aussies are slightly longer than tall. They are solidly built with moderate bone.

Aussies are athletes. They are attentive and animated, showing strength and stamina combined with unusual agility. The structure in the male reflects masculinity without coarseness. Bitches appear feminine without being slight of bone.

The Australian Shepherd is a medium-sized breed. Once all other qualities are brought into perspective, the importance of the Aussie's size is minimal against the appearance of the whole individual and the way in which he or she handles him or herself in action.

Unusual agility and working efficiency are based on sound, balanced structure and ability to pivot on the center line rather than size. Exceptions to the ideal size range should be faulted only to the degree of deviation, as with any other fault.

Test Your Judging I.Q. Size and Other DQs.

1. ☐ True ☐ False. The Australian Shepherd's height is measured from the ground to the highest point of the withers.

2. The withers are the:

   a. Upper tips of the scapula.
   b. 1st to the 9th thoracic vertebra.
   c. The highest point of the shoulders, behind the base of the neck.
   d. All the above.
   e. None of the above.

3. ☐ True ☐ False. Substance is determined by evaluating the amount of bone in the hind leg.

4. The Australian Shepherd is:

   a. Light and agile with fine bone.
   b. Solidly built with moderate bone.
   c. Solidly built with fine bone.
   d. Solidly built with heavy bone.

5. Unusual agility is due to:

   a. Medium size.
   b. Sound structure.
   c. Sound, balanced structure.
   d. Ability to pivot on centerline.
   e. "c." and "d."
   f. None of the above.

6. What is the size differentiation between males and females?

   a. Two inches.
   b. Four inches.
   c. One inch.
   d. Three inches.

7. ☐ True ☐ False. The preferred height is 20 to 23 inches for males and 18 to 21 inches for females in both ASCA and AKC.

8. What trait(s) is/are listed under "Other Disqualifications" in the ASCA Breed Standard?

   a. Undershot.
   b. Overshot.
   c. Wry mouth.
   d. Other than recognized colors.
   e. White body splashes.
   f. Dudley nose.
   g. Monorchidism.
   h. Cryptorchidism.

9. What is Monorchidism?

   a. Unilateral cryptorchidism.
   b. One retained testicle.
   c. One descended testicle.
   d. Bilateral cryptorchidism.

Answers Size and Other DQs.

1-True.

2-c. The highest point of the shoulders

3-True.

4-b.

5-e.

6-a.

7-True.

8-g. and h. Monorchidism and Cryptorchidism.

9-a, b or c. Monorchidism (only one testicle, has descended into the scrotum. Cryptorchidism (neither testicle has descended into the scrotum). Both monorchidism and cryptorchidism are disqualifications in ASCA. The AKC standard doesn't address these fundamentally serious hereditary faults.

☑ Judges Checklist

☑ **Keep in mind**: the Australian Shepherd's historical function is as a utilitarian breed developed in the ranch country of the American West.

☑ The Judges Approach

→ Move toward an Aussie evenly and without hesitation.
→ Approach from the front, so you don't startle an individual.
→ Speak calmly, use steady hands.
→ Knowledgeable judges should be able to observe an Aussie's expression without diverting the dog's attention from its handler using noisemakers.
→ Judges should know better, but floppy hats, loose clothing, reflective sunglasses, jingling keys and jewelry can cause some Aussies to react with concern and caution.
→ Hopefully the exhibit is trained and properly socialized, but an Aussie which will not stand for examination should be dismissed from the ring.

☑ General Appearance

→ Slightly longer than tall.
→ Medium size and bone.
→ Well balanced and athletic.
→ Coat of moderate length and coarseness.

☑ Temperament / Character

→ Aussies are extremely loyal and willing to please their owner, which is evident by their focus. Australian Shepherds are people oriented but reserved with strangers.
→ When properly socialized and trained, Aussies should be prepared to submit for examination in the show ring without being fearful or shy.

☑ Head

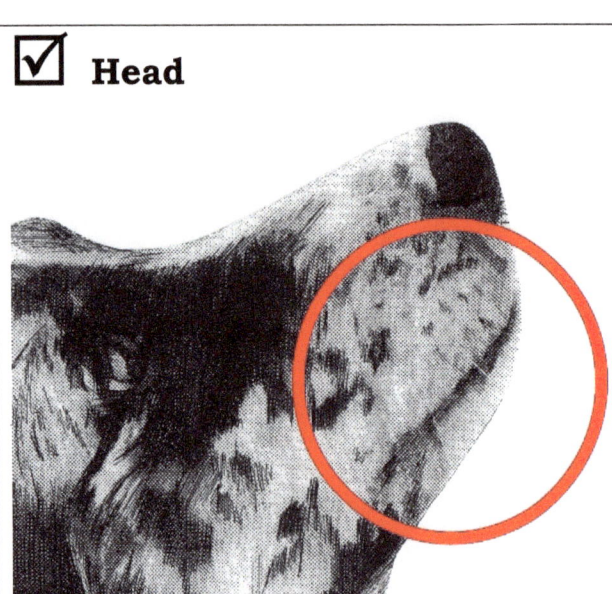

→ Clean-cut and dry. The lips are close-fitting and meet at the mouth line.
→ Skin around eyes close-fitting to form a tight, protective covering.
→ Stop is moderate, but well defined.
→ Sufficient under jaw.

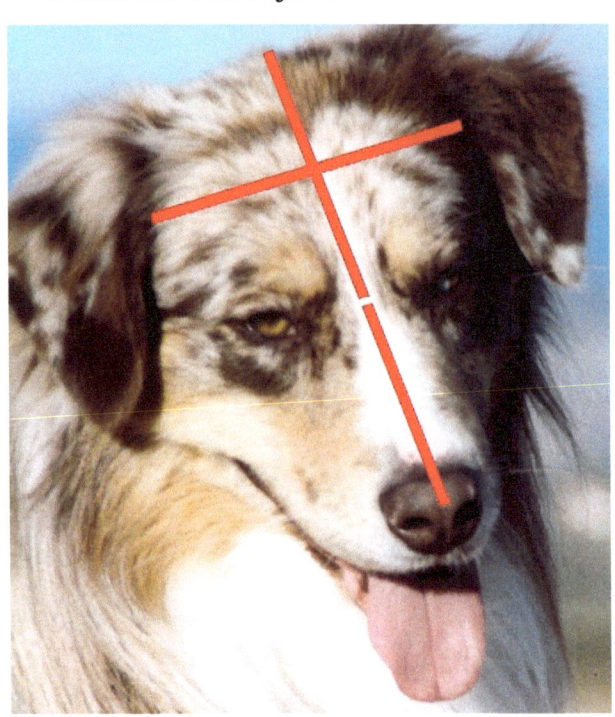

→ Look for balance. The length of the muzzle equals the length and width of the topskull.
→ The muzzle is of medium width and depth.

☑ Teeth

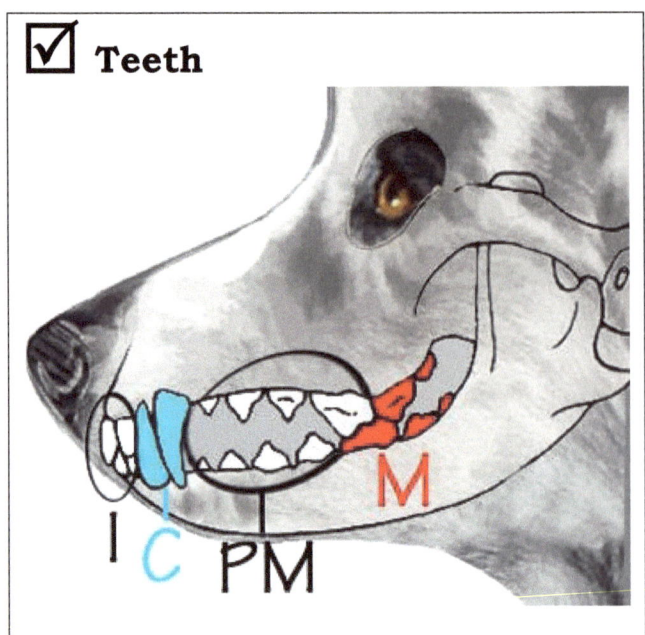

→ Full complement of teeth that meet in a scissors bite.

☑ Eyes

→ Almond shaped, of moderate size.
→ Expressive, showing attentiveness to their master or task.
→ A bright look reflects intelligence.

☑ Ears

→ Moderate size.
→ Should be useful and able to rotate ears from the front to the side or toward the rear to pick up sounds.
→ Ears lacking mobility are detrimental for utilitarian function.

→ It's not uncommon for an Aussie to have two different ears, one that breaks forward and the other breaks to the side. This is <u>not</u> a fault, but a unique part of expression.

☑ Neck, Topline, Body

→ Moderate bone.
→ Medium length neck, slightly arched at crest.
→ Muscular loin, strong and broad.
→ Moderately sloping croup.
→ Deep, well sprung ribs.
→ There should be **no** rolling across the topline.
→ As an athletic working breed, the Aussie should be physically fit with good muscle tone.
→ Tuck-up is visible and tapered.

→ What happens in the neck starts in the back, and what happens in the back starts in the hind legs. It's purely biomechanical.

☑ Forequarters

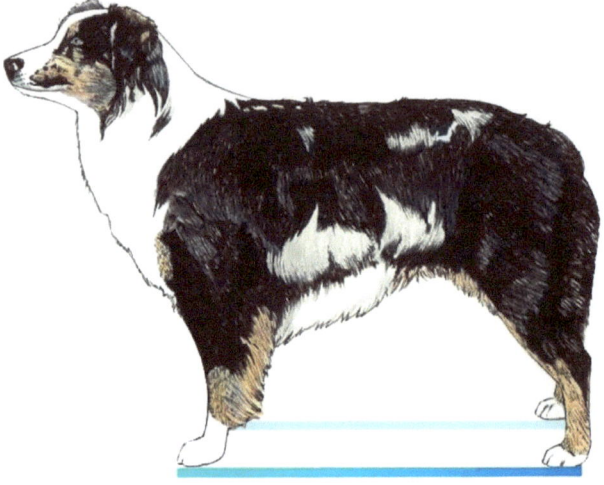

→ Natural four-square stance is the correct, normal stance for the breed.

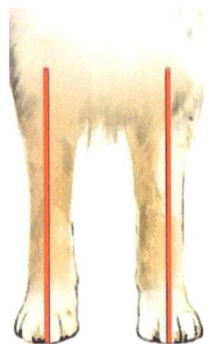

→ Forelegs are straight and perpendicular to the ground when viewed from the front.
→ It's normal for an Aussie to stand with the toes turned slightly to the sides as pictured above for stability. It is <u>not</u> the same as when the metacarpal bones are aligned outward causing the dog to "toe out" which is a fault.
→ Center of gravity passes along the radius and ulna to the pasterns to the feet.
→ Pasterns strong, but slightly sloped.
→ Oval shaped, modified hare-feet.
→ The heel or metacarpal pads must originate in a perpendicular line under the center of weight bearing.
→ "**No foot, no dog.**"

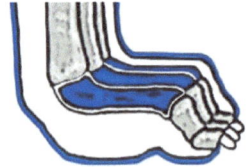

☑ Hindquarters

Trotting assembly.   Sprinting assembly.

→ The engine which provides energy and enables the dog to pivot sharply in turns.
→ Metatarsus and pads of the foot under the point of buttock (ischium) for linear stability, turn around efficiency and sudden gait changes.
→ Hock (tarsal) joint: moderately bent.
→ The width of the hindquarters (when viewed from behind) is equal to the width of the forequarters at the shoulders.
→ Legs should be equidistant from ground to elbow and elbow to the withers, but **not** shorter.
→ Slightly longer than shorter legs are more practical for the breed's function.
→ Oval shaped, modified hare-feet.

☑ Gait

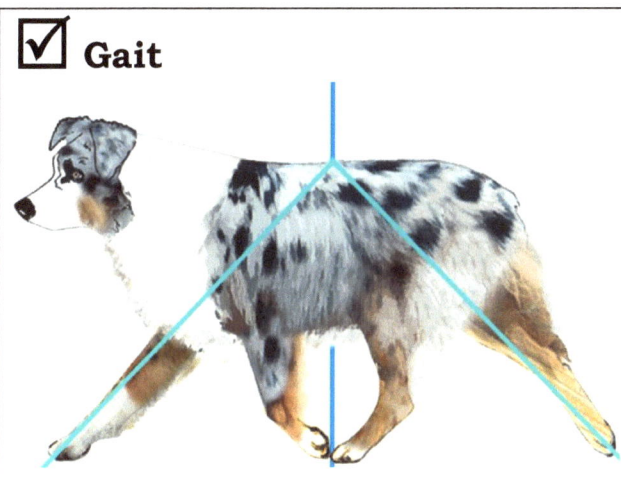

→ Aussies should be moved at a normal pace on a loose lead, not strung up.
→ The gait will be **balanced** when the angulation of the front assembly complements the angulation of the hindquarters.

☑ Down and Back

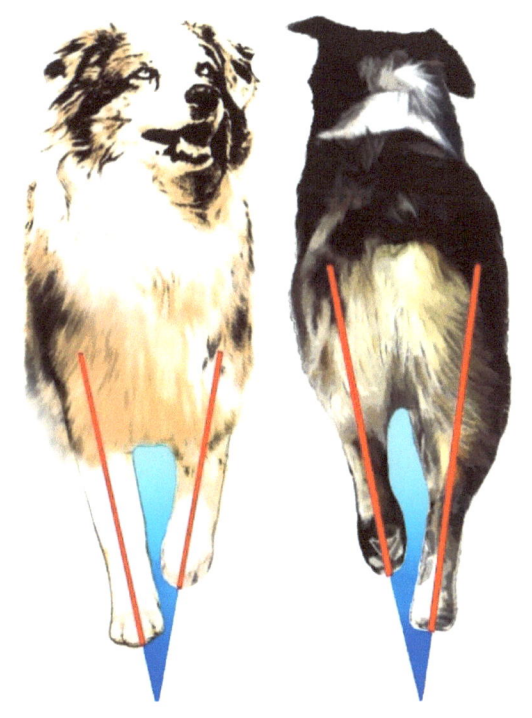

→ The legs converge towards the center line of gravity as speed increases.
→ Convergence formulates from the shoulder joint to the feet and from the hip joint to the feet.
→ The joints must not bend or twist when bearing weight in motion.

☑ Coat

→ Practical.
→ Moderate: kept or keeping within proper limits, not extreme or excessive.
→ Medium length and texture.
→ Moderately feathered.
→ Natural. Clean and neat, but not sculpted
→ Scissor marks and cut lines alters the natural coat and perhaps indicates an attempt to disguise an untypical coat which is to be severely faulted.

☑ Color

→ Deep, rich black or liver pigmentation
→ No color or pattern regardless how flashy or plain is preferred over another.
→ Remember, Solid or merle Aussies may appear <u>with or without</u> tan (copper) and/or white trim. One is not preferred over another.

☑ Color

→ None of the accepted colors (red or black) or patterns (merle) with or without white and/or tan trim is preferred over the others.
→ Markings may be symmetrical or asymmetrical without fault.

ASCA: On all colors the areas surrounding the ears and eyes are dominated by color other than white. The hairline (roots) of a white collar does not exceed the point at the withers.

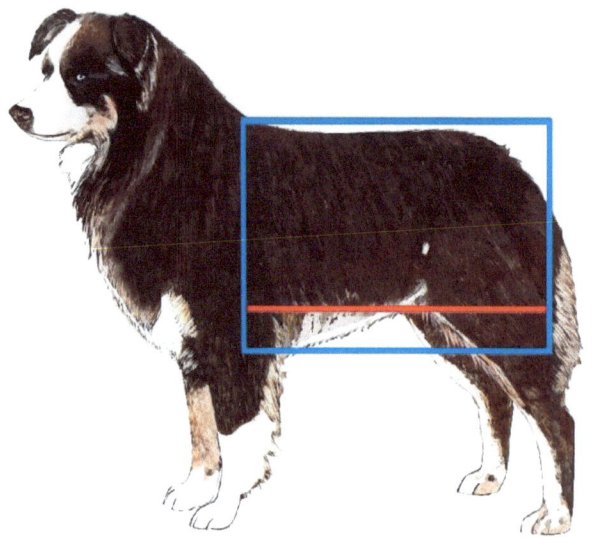

AKC: White is acceptable on the neck (either in part or as a full collar), chest, legs, muzzle, underparts, blaze on head and white extension from underpart up to four (4) inches (represented by the blue rectangle), measuring from a horizontal line at the elbow.

☑ Size

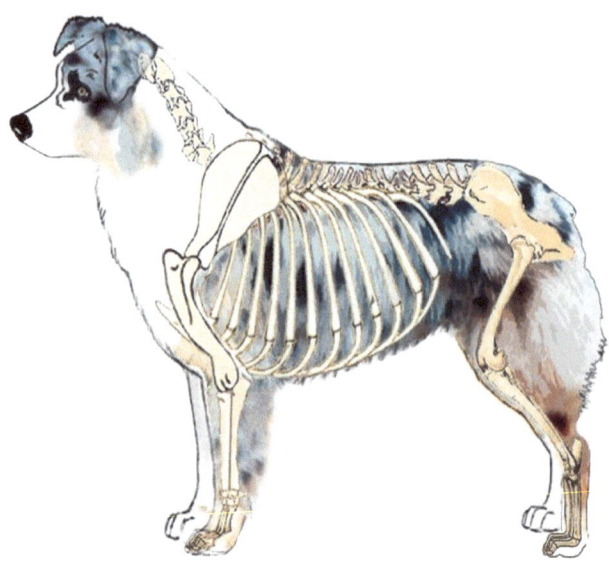

→ Medium size with moderate bone in proportion to the individual.
→ Preferred height for males is 20 to 23 inches.
→ Preferred height for females is 18 to 21 inches.
→ Quality is **never** to be sacrificed in favor of size.

☑ ASCA Disqualifications:

→ Undershot. Overshot, Wry mouth.

→ Other than recognized colors. White body splashes. Dudley nose.

→ Monorchidism and cryptorchidism.

☑ AKC Disqualifications:

→ Undershot, Overshot greater than 1/8th inch.

→ White body splashes, which means white on body (red rectangular area) between withers and tail, on sides between elbows and back of hindquarters in all colors.

Credits:

Carol Ann Hartnagle and Mike Ryan for their continued inspiration. Beth Anglemyer for proofreading the book. Images provided by American Veterinary Dental College, Gary Anderson Photography, Hartnagle Family Archive, Sue Bishop, Marsha Bain, Sherry Baker, Richard Bruner, Jennifer Cannon, Terri Carver, Deb Conroy, Sandy Cornwell, Lois George, Linda Gray, Cee Hambo, Jim Hartnagle, Gary and Mary Hawley, Silja Jonsson, Weldon T. Heard, Doug Mahan, Lisa Marshall, Anne Martin, Lucia Miller DVM, Heidi Mobley, Lynda Oleksuk, Adriana Plum, Rich Ruddish, Leslie Sharp, Trish Thornwald, Daniela Van der Lichte, Dorien Vogelaar, Kathy Warren, Sharon Watts, Tanya Wheeler, Vicki and David Whipp, Dave Whitaker, Phil Wildhagen, Judy Williams and Linda Wilson.

About the Author

Jeanne Joy (pictured above left in 1957) is uniquely qualified to talk about Australian Shepherds. She was born into the breed and has been judging Aussies since 1974. Jeanne served on the Breed Standard Committee for the Australian Shepherd Club of America from 1975 through 1977. She was one of the first five judges approved for ASCA's original Breeder Judge program in 1978. Additionally, Jeanne is an ASCA Stockdog Judge and an AKC Herding Trial Judge. Along with her family, she was recognized as ASCA's first Hall of Fame Kennel and the first ever Hall of Fame Excellent Kennel.

Furthermore, Jeanne Joy has authored numerous articles about the breed and several books, including **All About Aussies: The Australian Shepherd from A to Z**, now in its Fourth Edition.

For more information about the Australian Shepherd, please see her book, **All About Aussies: The Australian Shepherd from A to Z** and **The Total Australian Shepherd: Beyond the Beginning** by Carol Ann Hartnagle and Ernest Hartnagle.

www.ingramcontent.com/pod-product-compliance
Lightning Source LLC
Chambersburg PA
CBHW040730250426
43671CB00033B/41